TED BUNDY

THE YEARLY JOURNAL
VOLUME ONE - 2022

KEVIN SULLIVAN

WILDBLUE
PRESS

WildBluePress.com

TED BUNDY: The Yearly Journal Volume One published by:
WILDBLUE PRESS
P.O. Box 102440
Denver, Colorado 80250

WILDBLUE PRESS is registered at the U.S. Patent and Trademark Offices.

ISBN 978-1-957822-29-1 Hardcover
ISBN 978-1-957288-30-7 Trade Paperback
ISBN 978-1-957288-31-4 eBook

Cover design © 2022 WildBlue Press. All rights reserved.

Interior Formatting/Cover Design by Elijah Toten
www.totencreative.com

TED BUNDY

THE YEARLY JOURNAL
VOLUME ONE - 2022

TABLE OF CONTENTS

PREFACE

In late 2020, I completed *The Enigma of Ted Bundy*, my sixth book in a series about the life and murders of Ted Bundy. And if you've followed me throughout the years, you know that it all began with the publication of my first Bundy book, *The Bundy Murders: A Comprehensive History*; a book that I sincerely believed would be my one and only work on the case. Why did I believe this? Well, I was very fortunate during the writing of my first book to work with many of the people who were involved in the case, including the top investigators: Jerry Thompson out of Salt Lake City, Utah; Michael J. Fisher, the Colorado investigator; Russ Reneau and Randy Everitt, Idaho investigators; Robert D. Keppel, the Washington State investigator; Ira Beal, the Bountiful, Utah detective who worked the Carol DaRonch case; Don Patchen, the lead detective for the Tallahassee PD in the Florida Chi Omega murders; and Bill Hagmaier, the retired FBI agent from the Behavioral Science Unit who became very close with Bundy during the last years of his life, and spent as many as 200 hours interviewing the incarcerated killer.

It would be from these sources and the in-depth interviews that followed that new and never-before published information surfaced about several of the murders, along with new general information about the case. On top of this, I wrote the book from the perspective as if the readers were following Bundy's footsteps every step of the way. And the result was that *The Bundy Murders* became a best-selling book and remains so today. All of my writing about

Ted Bundy should have ended with the publication of my first book. I am glad that it didn't.

Of course, there are times when, unbeknownst to us, we'll begin traveling down a certain road and while we may believe it's only for a brief time, that road might continue with no end in sight. This is exactly what happened in the years following the publication of what I call today my main book on Ted Bundy. From that decision sprang five additional "companion" volumes. The first of these was *The Trail of Ted Bundy: Digging Up the Untold Stories* published in 2016; *The Bundy Secrets: Hidden Files on America's Worst Serial Killer* (2017); *Ted Bundy's Murderous Mysteries: The Many Victims of America's Most Infamous Serial Killer*, (2019); *The Encyclopedia of the Ted Bundy Murders* (2020). Also released in late 2020 was my sixth Bundy book, *The Enigma of Ted Bundy: The Questions and Controversies Surrounding America's Most Infamous Serial Killer*.

And of course, after *Enigma*, I was finally finished with Ted Bundy. Certainly, I reasoned, everything I wanted to say about the killer had surely been said. This Bundy series comprises over 1,400 pages, and that's a lot of writing, no matter how big and influential the case or the person may be. However, having put in so many years writing about Bundy has made me a sort of "point man" when it comes to those who either knew Bundy, knew the victims (or nearly became a victim themselves), and often they'll want to come forward to tell their stories, and many of these folks decide to contact me.

For example, from mid-January 2021 to February 1, 2021 (just two weeks), three women contacted me with stories of Ted Bundy. Out of the three, I believe one is absolutely a valid contact who had a run-in with the killer, and a second one may have as well. The last one did not have sufficient information (it came from her aunt, now deceased), and so

I did not follow it up with anything but a thank you for the contact.

So, the question becomes: do I simply bury this information to my voluminous Bundy case files, perhaps to never again see the light of day? That would make absolutely no sense, in my mind. And because of this, I've made the decision to never allow such information to be lost to the proverbial dustbin of history, and that I'll be writing a yearly update to the Bundy case, where new testimonies and new revelations will find a home. Remember, once these voices are stilled, fresh, first-person accounts will forever end. And sadly, it's already happening.

Over the last several years, we've lost important people connected to the Bundy case: Jerry Thompson, Bob Keppel, Dr. Al Carlisle, Ronald M. Holmes, Lorraine Fargo, and likely others of which I'm currently unaware. So, as long as I am here and folks are contacting me, I'll be bringing to the printed page all they tell me. I will also be delving into other aspects of the case that I feel are worthy of a closer investigation.

I can also assure you that what you'll be reading in this book will add even more important revelations concerning the life of Ted Bundy and the murders he committed. Indeed, the newest revelation (being published here for the first time) pertains to the identifying of Bundy's hunting ground for September 1974, that first month he arrived in Salt Lake City to attend law school. It's a fascinating discovery that frankly, I never expected to make. And yet, here we are…

TED BUNDY, RON HOLMES,
AND LOUISVILLE, KY

In my last book, *The Enigma of Ted Bundy*, I wrote about Ron Holmes, the late Louisville criminologist who worked with Bundy for a time prior to the killer's execution (I also included the transcript of the taped interview I conducted with Holmes in 2007). Although the two men exchanged many letters, Holmes interviewed Bundy for the better portion of a day in 1987 and had plans to return to the prison to do a filmed interview too—something which never occurred because of a disagreement between the two men causing the relationship to abruptly end. It is of interest to note too, that a number of years before I knew I'd be writing about the killer, I had the opportunity to read all of the letters Bundy mailed to Ron Holmes. (Unfortunately, I never made copies of these letters, as writing a book about Ted Bundy was not on my radar at the time). I have not read the letters Holmes sent to Bundy, but I do know these letters became the property of retired Washington State investigator Bob Keppel after Bundy's execution.

Most of what I wanted to say about the criminologist I said in *Enigma*, so nothing I say here will be a repeat of that information. However, there is additional material I would like to add that will be beneficial to the reader. It pertains to an article published in *The Courier-Journal* on October 5, 1986 by Ira Simmons, about the life and career of Holmes, and it's very enlightening, including the profiles Holmes provided to law enforcement over the years. One report, created in conjunction with Dr. Gary Sykes, aided Louisville detectives in nabbing Beoria Simmons, an African American serial killer of three African American women, and the information they provided proved to be extremely accurate. Without this profile, catching him would have been far more difficult.

Holmes also gave targeted information leading to the arrest of a Louisville serial rapist who had racked up twenty-eight attacks before he was apprehended. When Madisonville, Ky police found themselves at a dead end involving the gruesome murder of an elderly woman, and an attack on another elderly female they believed was committed by the same man, they turned to Holmes, who travelled to Madisonville to work up a profile on the unknown perpetrator. The victim, who had been stabbed 200 times and decapitated, had been killed, Holmes theorized, by someone who lived in the neighborhood, and gave police other suspected traits to look for. When captured, the culprit lived one block away and the profile fit him perfectly.

What follows are the highlights from the article relating to Ted Bundy. The original article was not in italics, but doing so here will aid readers as I'll be adding comments which appear in regular font.

THE ADVENTURES
OF DR. HOLMES

*A Louisville criminologist with a quiet demeanor
and name to live up to has made a reputation for
himself probing the dark mind of the serial killer*

By Ira Simmons

*His interview with Ted Bundy, he added, began on a
strangely down-home note. He asked Bundy if he had
driven through Louisville in 1978. Bundy said he had. "You
didn't stop, did you?" said Holmes. Bundy, he remembers,
smiled and said, "As a matter of fact, I did." On a cold
January morning eight years ago, Ted Bundy stopped at
the Chevron station at the southwest corner of Brook and
Jefferson Streets. After filling his tank, he had breakfast at
Uncle Hanks Pancake Cottage, 203 East Jefferson, now
site of the Chung King Chinese-American Restaurant...*
(Author's note: at the time I was living about eight miles
east of this location and just off River Road, and I would
pass Uncle Hanks Pancake Cottage often while driving into
downtown Louisville. When Bundy was here, the building
on the corner was either a Porter Paints store or soon would
be. Today, a larger building sits on this corner, and the
parking lot has gobbled up the lot where Uncle Hanks stood.
And if you visit the site today, you will see an automotive
garage in the rear and to the right of this parking lot, with
the sign emblazoned across the front, "Ted's Garage". The

winding exit ramp off of I-65 is still there, as is the building to the left of this ramp that was standing as Bundy passed it (Bundy would likely recognize it today). As Bundy took this exit, he saw the gas station on the corner and stopped for gas. He had likely already noticed Uncle Hanks to his right as he was descending the ramp, and because he had an affinity for pancake houses, he couldn't resist, circled the block, and went inside).

Breakfast in Louisville was a quiet moment in which he could rest and savor his new freedom. With all the violence behind him and the violence that lay ahead, he probably would not think much about his stop here until Holmes asked him about it with such intense curiosity.

"Ted," said Holmes, "you didn't stay long, did you?"

Bundy laughed.

Author's note: the article goes on to compare Holmes' work on and with serial killers to what other college and university professors do (non-violent studies), and it's followed by a revealing and honest quote about why he, and one could say all of us, are interested in the very dark world of serial murder:

This is a part of life that most people never see or pretend doesn't exist…I guess it's my way to legitimately look into the dark side of life. The mystery of violence repels and attracts. We're repelled by serial killers who have absolutely no conscience, yet we're fascinated by what they do, because it's so repulsive…maybe studying violence keeps me straight. I can see all this stuff without getting involved in it. Maybe it helps me feel I'm a nice guy. I have a dark side, as all of us do, but at least I'm not driven to express my darkness.

As to whether or not he thought Bundy was insane, Holmes hit the nail on the head when he said:

By no definition is Bundy insane. He knows right and wrong, but doesn't care.

In Holmes' book, *Serial Murder*, co-authored with James De Burger, he has a chapter on Ted Bundy and his many victims. He also includes his experience interviewing Bundy in person inside the Florida prison. What follows are some interesting insights Holmes gained from his interview and other interaction with Ted Bundy:

Ted offers important insight into the psychology of the serial killer. Most serial killers, he said, are people who kill for the "pure" pleasure of killing. The murder of another human being becomes such a psychological high that he has a "need" to repeat the killings again and again...the serial killer learns to stalk, wait, and kill, and with each killing he gets better in the stalking, the waiting, and the killing. Holmes said Bundy spoke of *the "force" (that) becomes so strong within the serial killer that he does not want to stop killing...there is a need deep within himself that demands that he kill, and the more he kills, the more he wishes to kill. The force is never satisfied.* Holmes, who had discussed Bundy's nature with Dr. Al Carlisle, said Carlisle referred to Bundy's secret part of his personality as the "beast", adding that Ted told him about "something deep inside me".

Before we leave Ron Holmes and Bundy's Louisville visit behind, it might be good to address why Bundy came through Louisville in the first place. In actuality, it was a mistake on Bundy's part—he simply took the wrong expressway. Bundy, a notoriously bad driver, would occasionally have directional issues, even when he had a map. And such was the case after he slipped into the driver's seat of a Japanese sedan that was sitting, keys in the ignition, at an auto repair shop that had closed for the day (the owners were no doubt planning to show up there the following morning to pick up their car). Although Bundy had already decided to head south to Florida, and consulted the appropriate maps, he still got lost and by his own admission, was late getting out of the city of Ann Arbor.

Now, there are two ways he could have driven to Florida, and both routes require one to take I-75 south out of Ann Arbor. The best route, of course, would have been I-75 south and that would take him through Lexington, Kentucky where he would continue on I-75 all the way through the state. This would have been the fastest way. However, because we know he came to Louisville, one of two things happened. Bundy either made a mistake and upon passing Lexington, and accidently took I-71 toward Louisville. Or, he may have made an even bigger mistake after he passed through Toledo, Ohio on I-75, and entered the on-ramp leading to I-69, meaning he was traveling in a south-westerly direction (and away from Florida) which would take him to Indianapolis, Indiana, greatly adding unnecessary time in his quest to get to Tallahassee. And in fact, this is what he may have done. Why do I say this? Well, we know that after Bundy left Ann Arbor, he drove for several hours (although it may have been a bit longer) before stopping to get some sleep. And if he made it all the way to Indianapolis, Indiana (or nearly so), he would only have a couple hours driving time coming through Indiana to reach the city of Louisville. And frankly, while it's a toss-up as to which route brought him to the city (we're in that dreaded place of speculation again), and because he ate breakfast at Uncle Hanks, I think he likely came from Indianapolis. And so, when writing *The Bundy Murders: A Comprehensive History*, I say that, *Early the next morning, Ted Bundy approached the Ohio River at Louisville. As he crossed the Kennedy Bridge which spans the river between Indiana and Kentucky...*

Am I correct about this? Perhaps; because Bundy did have breakfast in Louisville, making my Indianapolis hypothesis quite possible. And yet, there is no way (as far as I can tell) that we'll have a definitive answer to it; that is, unless Bundy made an obscure comment to someone somewhere, and it just hasn't yet come to light. One never knows when we're dealing with Ted Bundy, so it's best to never say never about such things.

Because I occasionally receive questions about Holmes and the books he's co-authored, I will include them here, and these can be found on Amazon. Because Holmes and I lived in the same city, his books show up in local Half Price bookstores in Louisville for a fraction of the cost online.

Profiling Violent Criminals: An Investigative Tool December 1, 2008

by Ronald M. Holmes, Stephen T. Holmes

Sex Crimes: Patterns and Behaviors June 18, 2008

by Stephen T. Holmes, Ronald M. Holmes

Fatal Violence: Case Studies and Analysis of Emerging Forms April 19, 2016

by Ronald M. Holmes, Stephen T. Holmes

Suicide: Theory, Practice and Investigation July 27, 2005

by Ronald. M. Holmes, Stephen T. Holmes

Introduction to Gangs in America April 24, 2012

by Ronald M. Holmes, Richard Tewksbury, George Higgins

Current Perspectives on Sex Crimes December 20, 2001

by Ronald M. Holmes, Stephen T. Holmes

Serial Murder September 1988

by Ronald M. Holmes, James De Burger

Sex Crimes: Patterns and Behaviors November 6, 2001

by Ronald M. Holmes, Stephen T. Holmes

BUNDY'S FAILED ABDUCTIONS

Although we don't know the exact number of women and girls Bundy murdered (he admitted to 30, but the authorities believe the total is far more), conservative estimates run anywhere from the mid- to upper-30s, while some posit it's likely over one hundred. Personally, I lean to the conservative end, but many believe that past the 30 to 36 victims count is a more accurate figure. My thinking is somewhere close to 40 or perhaps as many as 45; although I acknowledge it could go higher. I believe it goes beyond the standard number of 36 because while Bundy didn't mind admitting to the murders of college-age women, he never wanted to talk about the murders of young teenage girls, or (shocking though it is), the killing of pre-teens. We know he murdered Lynette Culver of Pocatello, Idaho and Kimberly Leach of Lake City, Florida, both of whom were 12-years-old. But in my mind there has to be more, and here's why:

During one of Bundy's third-person confessions prior to his true, end-of-life confessions of murder, he mentioned a serial killer (himself) who was responsible for the deaths of a half dozen young girls. So, whatever the true number happens to be, we can all safely say there are more murder victims he's responsible for than the total he gave at the end. Indeed, he admitted to Bill Hagmaier he doesn't even know the real number.

Well, let's look at some other numbers; numbers that, in my view, run from large to possibly very high. And while it's speculation (something I always try to avoid), it's only speculation as to the actual numbers. And this isn't the first time I've speculated, or theorized, about a particular aspect pertaining to the Bundy case, *if* there is strong circumstantial evidence surrounding it.

Now, because I've been researching and writing about Ted Bundy for the last 16 years, I've pondered many aspects of the case and occasionally I'll feel confident about the possibility of filling in the blanks where our knowledge of Bundy's actions remains unknown; that is, he never talked about them. These, of course, must be rightly categorized as speculations or theories, that while unprovable, end up making a great deal of sense; at least, a great deal of sense to me. I presented a couple of these theories in my sixth book, *The Enigma of Ted Bundy*. To name two examples for those who haven't read the book, I mention my theory that Bundy intentionally began killing in the middle of the night and gradually, because he felt more confident, slowly began hunting women in the daylight, and the boldest daylight attack was at Lake Sammamish on the sunny Sunday of July 14, 1974.

However, after Lake Sammamish, where he abducted two women several hours apart and was both seen and heard by a number of people, went back into hunting at night for the next nine months. Why did he do this? Well, making himself so visible led to composite drawings being made, and those who overheard him and watched him speak with and lead Janice Ott out of the park, came forward and told the authorities what they had said to one another. Not only this, but one potential victim, Janice Graham, who followed him to his car but did not go with him, told police he was driving a beige VW and explained where it was parked. He was also heard introducing himself to Janice Ott as "Ted".

Why would he expose himself to the public in such ways? Bundy was not only extremely arrogant, but he'd been on his successful and uninterrupted trail of murder since January of that year—almost seven months! He believed he could get away with anything, and up till now he'd been correct. But Bundy, coming down from his "high" from the successful lake murders, began to see that he had opened an investigative door that could be problematic.

The other theory (again, based on good circumstantial evidence) is the idea that Bundy kept the money (dollars and change) of the victims he killed, because he was always broke. It was a theory I first posited on my Facebook page and published in more detail in the book.

I will present another unprovable (as to actual numbers) theory that for every woman Bundy was able to lead away and kill, there may be anywhere from 10 to 30 women or young girls he attempted to abduct that escaped his trap, and these women or young girls likely had no idea they were ever in danger.

Statistically speaking, this has to be true in many of his murders, even if it's on the lower end of ten. Indeed, Bundy himself admitted there were times when no matter how hard he tried (and he's speaking of many hours of hunting), he came up empty of victims, and only he knew the number of potential victims he spoke to on any given hunt. So, what does all of this mean and how can we possibly discover a fairly accurate estimate of these once-potential victims of Ted Bundy? Well, let's look at what I believe are the likely numbers.

For our purposes, let's say Bundy's total homicide count stands at 35. Then, let's posit on average he might speak with only ten women each time to abduct one, then we have a total contact number of 350 women or young girls. Now, that's quite a number, and yet, I still think it's likely too low. Of course, some victims were crimes of opportunity (think hitchhikers), and these women would not factor into the equation of a purposeful hunt as she was in essence seeking a ride and it took no special effort on his part to obtain her. And yet, we know he talked to many at Lake Sammamish on July 14, 1974, and we also know by Bundy's own words that he spent the day of May 6, 1975 in Pocatello, Idaho, hunting coeds but came up empty-handed; and we're likely talking many hours from mid-day until sometime after dark. The same is true when Bundy visited Central Washington State College, on two different days, and the only person he abducted from the campus was Susan Rancourt on April 17, 1974.

How many did Bundy actually have contact with at CWSC? We don't know. But because he spent many hours there on the 17th (he was hunting in the afternoon until approximately 10:30 p.m. at which time he convinced Rancourt to follow him to his car), he may have had several dozen that day alone. Keep in mind too, that my figure of 10 per victim is almost certainly on the low side. Ted Bundy coming up without victims happened a lot. And if we raise his failures above the number 10, at least for some of his hunts, then perhaps it's as many as 400 potential victims, or more, that Ted Bundy approached with the idea of killing them.

Because we're attempting to obtain new information, in the recent Bundy film, *No Man of God*, based on the tapes, transcripts, and recollections of Bill Hagmaier, Bundy said there were several of his victims who woke up after being bashed in the head and dragged from his car, and some of these women came to and were able to escape into the woods when he wasn't looking (he mentioned 'going after his tools' at one point). When pressed as to how many he really murdered, he wanted to settle on 30. But when pressed again by Hagmaier, he admitted he didn't know. It's likely had he been asked about all the women he attempted to abduct, and it's likely the number is so great even he would have no idea. It should be noted too that Bill Hagmaier was closely associated with the film, and these confessions are taken either from tapes, taped transcripts, or from the notes and remembrances of Hagmaier himself.

What follows are additional stories that have surfaced over the last several years (and some very recently), that I will be using for the very first time. As a preface to these, I would like to remind readers that on rare occasions (perhaps only a few times), Bundy would convince a woman to go with him to his car, and despite his very real intention of killing her moments before, would simply change his mind and let her go on her way. One incident that stands out is his attempted abduction of a woman in the U-District (the same location where he would abduct George Hawkins less than two weeks later), but for some odd reason, when they reached his car, he changed his mind and simply thanked her and allowed her to walk away. What really bothered Bundy (he explains all of this on tape), is that after the Hawkins murder, he was afraid this woman might come forward and tell the cops about him, his feigning injury, and that he mentioned that he lived in the area. She also saw the make and color of his car. So it makes sense Bundy was a bit alarmed about it.

If Bundy were here today, he might not be able to tell you exactly why he let her go, but apparently, that overwhelming desire to murder instantly vanished. Perhaps it was something she said, or something he perceived about her; we just don't know. But one thing we do know is that the "entity" or that overwhelming desire to kill that Bundy often referred to, was suddenly missing. Knowing this, let us pay special attention to what Bundy told Stephen Michaud in a Q&A between author and killer and is found in *Ted Bundy: Conversations with a Killer*, by Stephen Michaud and Hugh Aynesworth:

To set the scene, Michaud wanted to know if Bundy had ever picked up a girl he didn't intend on murdering, and he asked him to speak about "this killer" and what the killer might do. And Bundy, speaking in the third-person about what he actually did, understood that "confessing" this to Michaud could never be used against him. Without question, what he's saying here about those desires to murder are very real and that it's not a static condition; that is, it can rise or fall and it's clear Bundy could tell where "he" was in this situation at any moment during the process.

TB: He was in one of his reformation periods, (a laugh). He'd sworn to himself that he'd never engage in that kind of conduct again. That he wouldn't let himself be carried away like that. But when he was faced with this very attractive girl hitchhiking, it kind of presented a challenge. He didn't look on it as a challenge but as an opportunity; it was sort of an ambiguous situation.

SM: It seems as if his normal self was responding positively to her.

TB: Uh huh. That would be fair to say. The sexual activity was very responsive and very energetic. Uh, at certain parts of the evening he felt himself on the edge of taking her life, just, just out of the desire to do so. But the justifications were not there. Nor was that malignant condition that active at that time. It was active, but not at high strength. But when morning came around and they dressed and he took the girl back to the area where she lived, he felt like he'd accomplished something. He deluded himself at that point into thinking that he had really conquered those impulses. But within a period of time he discovered that that was an inaccurate conclusion. He didn't recognize then, or perhaps he did not want to recognize, that just the matter of a week or two later he probably would have killed her.

What follows are some interesting, "almost" victims of Ted Bundy...

AN ENCOUNTER AT OREGON STATE UNIVERSITY

Several years ago, I was contacted by a woman who believed she'd had an encounter with Bundy at Oregon State University in Corvallis, Oregon. Of course, she didn't know who he was until a few years later after his picture was splashed all over the newspapers and on television.

As we talked about what happened, it had, in my mind, all the earmarks of being Ted Bundy. I then asked if she could determine what year this occurred, and she said the early 1970s. When asked if there was any way she could narrow it down, she said she'd do some checking and get back with me. When she messaged me again, she stated it happened in 1973 (*it's possible she said 1975, but because the message is now lost, I can't say with absolute certainty. Even so, I do believe it's '73. In either case, because Bundy wasn't arrested until August of 1975, either date still rules him in as a possibility*), as she was able to correlate it with something else that took place around the same time. Regrettably, I then said it couldn't have been Bundy, as he'd traveled to the school in 1974, and that resulted in the late-night abduction and murder of Kathy Parks. My thought was perhaps she was an earlier intended victim that same day, perhaps in the afternoon. Once I burst her bubble, she (unfortunately!) seemed convinced it wasn't Bundy after all. A simple mistake on her part, I believed.

And then, about six months ago, I was speaking with Mike McCann, a friend and fellow Bundy researcher, and he mentioned Bundy murdered two women in Oregon and it's like I was hearing it for the first time. However, when I returned to my files, I located an FBI report that Bundy confirmed he killed two in Oregon, and somehow it had slipped my mind. Now, had I only remembered this while conversing with my contact, I wouldn't have foolishly deleted her post! Unfortunately, when I went back into my electronic files to retrieve our discussion, I couldn't locate it. And while I rarely delete such conversations, it's possible I did just that. Even so, I remember enough of our conversation to give you at least an idea why she originally believed it was Ted Bundy, and why I now think she was correct.

As I said, it was in broad daylight, and Bundy was apparently driving slowly through the Oregon State University campus, looking at the females he was passing. And then something occurred and she mentioned that she nearly bumped into his VW when she stepped into the street, wherein some conversation between the two ensued. In classic Bundy style, I remember she said he asked her to get into his car, but unfortunately, what the actual conversation was I can no longer remember. And while it was a brief back and forth between them, it was enough time for her to get a really good look at the man and remember his voice. Plus, she accurately described his make of car, a VW—and its color. It is of interest to note too, that Bundy purchased his 1968 beige VW Bug in 1973.

Do I believe it was Bundy? Well, while we'll never know for a certainty, I think it was likely Bundy, and I know she certainly thought so after he was finally revealed. And now that I have refreshed my memory with the FBI document that states he admitted to murdering two in the state, in my mind, it's extremely likely because Bundy was a creature of habit, like stopping at the same places for gas when he was out of town and on the hunt, that he may, in fact, have trolled the campus on two occasions, even if he obtained that second victim elsewhere in the state. One caveat where Mike and I *may* differ (and I emphasize may), is that he believes Bundy killed two in Oregon but he does not include Kathy Parks in that total. He knows Bundy killed Parks, but he leaves that murder out of the equation, and I will not be saying why this is, as you'll read about it in his upcoming book. Needless to say, I will never again discard any information or communication I receive on this case, even when I believe it's likely I'll never use it.

A QUICK TRIP HOME
TO SEATTLE

I believe it was about eight years ago that a woman contacted me looking for some answers about an encounter she had with a man in Seattle around the first week in June 1975. She said she believed it was Ted Bundy who rolled up to her as she was walking down a Seattle sidewalk, and that he started up a conversation with her. It was during the day and she apparently wasn't afraid something might happen, but Bundy being Bundy, was soon asking her to get into his car and that was not something she was not going to do.

When she first mentioned this had happened in June '75, I wasn't sure it could have been Bundy as he'd been killing in Utah and the surrounding states since the fall of 1974 through the period where she was now claiming he was trying to abduct her in Seattle. Well, I told her I'd check my book, *The Bundy Murders: A Comprehensive History* to see if I could locate anything on Bundy traveling to Seattle during the month of June and once I checked, Eureka! I discovered Bundy did in fact return home on June 6, 1975, and I believe he was there for about a week.

Once discovered, I contacted her to confirm Bundy was in Seattle that June, that he was there around the first week of the month, and given what she'd said about him (what he looked like, his VW, and what she said to his repeated requests to get into his car), I told her she likely had an encounter with the killer.

Because our communication was a few years after my Bundy book was published, and I had no intention of writing another book on the case, I didn't obtain any additional contact information from her. Nor did I file the info for future use as believed I wouldn't need it. Of course, once I decided to write my second book, *The Trail of Ted Bundy: Digging Up the Untold Stories*, I carefully filed each contact that I believed was an actual almost Bundy victim. Nevertheless, I'm happy to present her story here.

BUNDY, A HUNTER
OF YOUNG GIRLS

In my book, *The Enigma of Ted Bundy*, I told the story of Michele Komen Nelson, an almost-victim of Ted Bundy. She was just a child of 14 when Bundy tried to get her into his car one morning as she was walking alone to her bus stop in Seattle. I won't go into the entire story here, other than to say that what she said he said is again, classic Bundy. It seems that no matter what verbal ruses Bundy used to try to convince women or young girls to get into his car, he had a way of saying it, making them clearly recognizable. When one begins to compare his "opening lines" to the various women he encountered while hunting, it's very clear Bundy never deviated all that much when he was presenting a ruse to his potential victims.

Anyway, after the book was published, I received a call from Bundy researcher, Mike McCann, and he said he'd read Michele's story in my book and had some information for me. That information was a statement given by a bus driver to the police telling of a 14-year-old girl who'd been frightened by a man who was trying to get her into his VW. The report continues to describe the car and its blemishes, and apparently this fit with Bundy's VW at that time. This young girl, who is unnamed in the report, (a report taken, Mike told me, by Detective Randy Hergesheimer), believes he followed her from her home.

As we discussed this, he mentioned he believed this must be referring to Michele Komen. I immediately agreed as they appeared to be so similar. To be sure, I said I'd contact Michele and let her know what's been found. At this point, I felt it had to be her as it appeared to be in the same neighborhood, and the age was correct. However, as soon as she viewed the report, she said it wasn't her, adding that while this incident occurred quite near to where Bundy attempted to abduct her, it was not the same area. Plus, while Michele was attending Thompson Junior High, this unknown girl was a student at Wilson Junior High.

This means that, for whatever reason, Bundy was intentionally hunting very young girls, and in fairly close proximity to one another. It's just a small circumstantial leap to conclude that there might be other young girls in the Seattle area who might have had similar odd experiences with Bundy, but never reported it.

This doesn't surprise me, of course, as I've believed for years Bundy killed far more young girls than just Kimberly Leach and Lynette Culver, both of whom were 12. That said, reading this report of the attempted kidnapping of a child, in an area very close to where Michele Komen encountered Bundy, did give me a dose of the cold chills.

GLORIA THORNE

I was recently contacted by a nice woman by the name of Gloria Thorne. The reason for her reaching out to me was, as you might suspect, to tell me of her encounter with Ted Bundy; an encounter, by the way, that took place in either 1970 or 1971 in North Tacoma—an area that Bundy knew well. What follows is her communication to me through Facebook Messenger. Gloria's comments are in italics:

Hi Mr. Sullivan, my name is Gloria and I'm a 69 years old woman who had a run in with Ted Bundy back in the early 70s in the north end of Tacoma, WA where his mother lived. I know the ruse he used to get girls into his car, because I almost did...

It was either '71 or '72. This was long before Ted Bundy was ever heard of. I was walking to Hanks Tavern so I was on about north 6th and L Street. Man pulled up to me in a blue/black El Camino...he was facing opposite direction from me (Author's note: it has become clear through my many years of research that Bundy borrowed cars far more frequently than most people suspect. And in this particular incident, Bundy, of necessity, would have had to borrow someone's vehicle, as he wouldn't purchase his prized beige VW Bug until 1973.)

He asked me for directions to a famous landmark restaurant in Tacoma. I started to tell him, and he said he was late for a meeting and would I ride with him and show him how to get there. He said he would give me taxi money to get back. Normally, I would have jumped at the chance...party money for me and my friends. I walked over and put my hands on the car door to open and get in. I remember thinking where do I sit as the bucket seat was gone. I looked at him and it was like something slapped me...I was immediately frightened and said no and walked away. Three days later, the same man, same car, same thing happened to my friend Pam. Years went by and I was at my mother's house, the paper (newspaper) *was there and I saw a picture of the man I had the encounter with. That was the first time I learned of Bundy.*

In my return message, I asked Gloria a number of questions, including the name of the 'landmark' restaurant, and here is her response: *Pam had the same encounter in the north end of Tacoma not far from where I did. Hank's tavern is at North K Street. That's where we all met up at. I was just 21, and wore my hair long and parted in the middle. The landmark restaurant was Top of the Ocean. Everyone in Tacoma knew where it was...I lost touch with Pam around 1974 when she moved to California. I have no idea where she would be, and never got a chance to talk about Bundy with her. I never contacted the police, I just figured he was already arrested and I probably wouldn't have been listened to. When I first saw his picture in the paper, I really wasn't aware of the extent of his crimes, especially around the Lake Sammamish area, I just recognized his face.*

Mike McCann, who is both a friend and fellow Bundy researcher who lives in Tacoma, is not only familiar with Hank's Tavern (he loved the place), but he lived in that area of north Tacoma years ago. When we were texting about this (yes, we often share our "finds"), he mentioned that where she encountered Bundy at 6th and L streets, there was a Bavarian restaurant that Bundy liked, and it was here where Bundy had a meal with his cousin, John Cowell, soon after he murdered Kathy Parks. It should also be noted that Bundy's parents, living at 3214 North 20th Street, were in fact very close to both the restaurant and where Bundy attempted to abduct Gloria Thorne.

A KNOCK AT THE DOOR

On December 28, 2016, I received an interesting Facebook communication, and as you might be thinking right about now, it had to do with Ted Bundy. It was from a woman who, in 1975, was living at 603 First Avenue in Salt Lake City, Utah, right down the block from Ted Bundy, whose apartment was at 565 First Avenue. Her message was short and to the point: she said that one night Bundy knocked on her door, but she refused to answer it, adding that her life was spared by her Great Dane, Nora, who was presumably barking its head off. She also mentioned Bundy was arrested within weeks of this incident. Is any of this possible? Absolutely.

Most people think that Bundy, while prowling neighborhoods, would go from one place to another almost aimlessly, until he found a victim walking down the street, stopped and abducted her, and that did happen. However, Bundy would also stalk women as well. He'd make mental notes of where they lived so he could return at another time and perhaps in the middle of the night, enter the dwelling and do a search of the house. But Bundy would also admit to knocking on women's apartment doors in the middle of the day, and these, of course, would be women he'd either observed living there or perhaps followed them home. For some reason he targeted them and we have no idea how often it happened.

When Bundy attacked Cheryl Thomas in her Dunwoody duplex (after attacking the women at Chi Omega) in the wee hours of February 15, 1978, authorities believed it was no accident that he went straight to her address. They believe he'd been there prior to the attack, and that he knew exactly where he was going after leaving the carnage of Chi Omega behind. Cheryl Thomas, interviewed for the Oxygen Bundy documentary, *Snapped: Notorious Ted Bundy*, mentioned Bundy looked familiar and added she might have seen him riding a bicycle past her house one day. If this is true, there's no telling just how many times he approached her duplex prior to the attack of February 15th. And so, I think it's fair to posit that whatever happened, Bundy began fixating on her and his obsession was not going to stop until he had her. So too, I believe the above story appears to be true as well, and that's why I've included it here.

ANOTHER KNOCK
AT THE DOOR

An interesting thing happened just as I was finishing up the previous story about Bundy knocking on the door at 603 First Avenue, because this second contact claimed that her mother also got a knock on her door, and it too was Ted Bundy. But this time, the door would be opened and Bundy found himself facing two women. Those women, Debbie Christenson and Frieda Aid, both of whom were friends and had moved from Florida together to Salt Lake City in July 1974, rented a place in the Annie Laurie Apartments, located at 135 E 300 S Salt Lake City, which still stands today. What follows is their story, which I received from Jodi Jones Basham, Debbie Christenson's daughter, and from Frieda Aid during our phone conversation on May 25, 2021.

Although not as close to our previous story's location (on a map, it's five blocks west of Bundy's apartment and then three blocks south), according to MapQuest, the various travel times between Bundy's place and the Annie Laurie Apartments (these are nice brownstones) is as follows: it's a four-minute drive by car from here to Bundy's 565 apartment, a 27-minute walk, or a nine-minute bike ride. In any event, it's well within the range of Bundy's normal activities (hunting and non-hunting) where he could spot someone walking or entering her apartment, and decide to abduct her at another time. I've been all over this area both in 2006 when I did my original research for my book, *The*

Bundy Murders: A Comprehensive History, and again in 2015 for my book, *The Trail of Ted Bundy: Digging Up the Untold Stories*, and Bundy was apparently crisscrossing this area a lot, beginning sometime after his September 3, 1974 arrival in Salt Lake City. Nevertheless, here's the story of Debbie Christenson as told by her daughter, Jodi:

Back in the 1970s my mom was living in an apartment with her college roommate in Salt Lake City. One night a man knocked on their door and her roommate answered it. It was a nice-looking man and he asked if a specific girl lived in their apartment building. My mom and her roommate did not know this girl but as he described her, they thought of another girl in the building. They told him they thought they had seen her in the parking garage a few times. He said he was asking because he was in her law class at the University of Utah and had borrowed her notes and was wanting to return them to her. My mom offered to give them to her when she saw her next but the man said no it was alright, he would give them to her the next day in class... (Author's note: this is typical Bundy; that is, making up a rather absurd excuse on the fly and then turn right around, saying he could give her the notes "the next day in class"; something that could raise suspicions leaving the listener thinking "if you could give them to her tomorrow, why are you looking for her now?". This was not the first time Bundy suddenly let loose a lame excuse to cover why he was doing something that might appear weird, but lucky for him, this did not set off any alarms in the two young women.)

...My mom said he was very nice. He left after that. A little bit later, I'm not sure how long, it wasn't (long) until my mom and her roommate saw on the news that Ted Bundy was captured and they realized it was the same man who had knocked on their door that day. Then they remembered they had seen his Volkswagen Beetle (sic) *car parked on their street a few times and driving past quite often as well.*

(Author's note: when Jodi says it wasn't long until her mom and Frieda saw that Bundy had been arrested, that's likely an honest mix-up on her mom's part, as Frieda (as you'll see in her comments below) is absolutely sure this occurred prior to the "murders in October", meaning before October 1974.)

Without question, Bundy parking in neighborhoods and getting out and walking around had been a common occurrence for him, not just here in Utah, but back in Washington State. We must remember that while Bundy could be an excellent planner of murder, he was also an opportunist. And when he spotted an opportunity in the making, he would race to it like a shark catching the scent of blood in the water.

What follows is from my conversation with Frieda Aid, and her testimony brings additional light concerning the woman Bundy was looking for. Please note that the brownstone in which they lived had several floors and Frieda and Debbie lived on the ground floor.

Frieda said that when they opened the door, the first thing out of Bundy's mouth was, "I'm sorry to bother you…", which was classic Bundy when attempting to beguile his victims into following him. Some of the other known niceties were: "Excuse me, miss…"; or "Could you please help me?"; "or Excuse me, young lady…"; or, in response to an offer of help, "Yeah, could you?". All so innocent. All so deadly. True, he wasn't hunting these two women, as he had his sights on someone else. Even so, the ruse was working perfectly.

Frieda said Bundy began asking about a young woman who lived in the building and as he described her, Frieda believed she knew who he was talking about. She was a telephone operator who worked nights, and because Frieda and Debbie worked days, they sometimes passed each other when they were coming home and the woman was leaving for work. When I asked Frieda to describe her, she said the woman was pretty and had long dark hair, which was something we know Bundy liked. I asked if there was anything about Bundy's demeaner which bothered her (were his eyes funny looking or weird, etc.), and she said no. On the contrary, they both called him really good looking and he was acting both nice and normal. Nothing about him in any way gave them pause, and as Frieda confessed, she's such an extrovert, she's surprised she didn't ask him in for dinner.

When I inquired as to when in 1974 this occurred, she believed it was before the murders began in October; the first being, of course, that of Nancy Wilcox, 16, on October 2nd. It is interesting to note another attempted abduction that occurred in September '74 happened when Bundy tried to convince Susan Milner, who also lived (like Bundy), in the "Avenues", to take a ride with him, and she declined (you can read her full story in my book, *The Enigma of Ted Bundy*). So, it's clear Bundy was very busy even in the areas that were very close to where he lived and attended law school.

Lastly, do I believe this was Ted Bundy? In this case, I absolutely do. I will not be using words here like "likely" or "probably", as they just wouldn't fit. There is absolutely no question in my mind that it was Bundy, and both women easily recognized him once his picture was plastered across the local news broadcasts and the daily papers after Bundy was charged with the kidnapping of Carol DaRonch in October 1975. And personally, I'm very surprised that Bundy, as soon as he arrived in the city on September 3, 1974, almost immediately began hunting women. And I'm even more surprised that instead of branching out a fairly good distance from where he lived, he was searching for prey within mere blocks of his 565 First Avenue apartment.

We can also assume these two incidents were not the only incidents in "The Avenues" that September; and in fact, until Bundy's arrest, the area in which he lived was still a place to hunt, as evidenced by the knock on the door at 603 First Avenue just a few weeks prior to his arrest. It is also important to note, that when I was writing *The Bundy Murders: A Comprehensive History*, I became aware of other incidents that I found in the Salt Lake City papers, (some intriguing, others not), that may have in fact been Ted Bundy. And of course, I found the same type of incidents in the Seattle papers when I was researching the murders there. But because I was writing the story of Bundy's life, and all the known murders he committed, I didn't follow the "what if" trails of these women and concentrated on his actual victims. Even so, over the years I would hear from many folks who knew Bundy, knew his victims, were involved in the case one way or another, or fortunately escaped him. And all of these testimonies have gone into the various companion volumes I've penned over the span of the sixteen years I've been writing about the case.

Since I was fortunate to obtain the Susan Milner story in time for my last book, *The Enigma of Ted Bundy*, where she was asked by Bundy to take a ride with him as she sat in a swing set on a school grounds only blocks from Bundy's apartment house, and have since learned about Bundy's stalking women in and around the Annie Laurie Apartments just a bit farther from where Milner encountered him, it became clear to me (for the first time, I might add) that Bundy's first hunting of women in the state began very close to home, and in areas swarming with people. It's also evident from these two encounters that Bundy (and this may have been for specific reasons known only to him), was moving in a westerly and south westerly direction and away from the nearby university which is east of his rooming house.

Although I don't like speculation unless it's backed by what I consider fairly good circumstantial evidence, it might be that Bundy purposely stayed away from the campus because the chances of being recognized by people he'd recently met. No guarantee about the validity of this theory, mind you, but currently all the testimonies I have gathered, have Bundy moving in that westerly direction. Even so, no matter the current lack of evidence, we can't say for a certainty Bundy didn't look for victims east of his apartment, which would bring him closer to the University of Utah, but so far, I don't have anything to put him in that direction during that first month he was there. As mentioned earlier, his ringing of the door at 603 First Avenue was slightly east of his apartment, but that occurrence did not happen until 1975 and only weeks before his arrest. And for me, the most surprising aspect of his September 1974 hunting mode is not that he was looking either east or west, but that this bold killer actually felt comfortable hunting so incredibly close to where he laid his head down at night! To the normal mind (something Bundy didn't possess), it would be far more prudent and exceedingly safer to begin hunting women at a far greater distance away from "home territory" where we now know he chose to operate. That Bundy began his first attempted abductions in what can be considered his own backyard says a great deal about his contempt for society and the authorities. With even this incredibly bold move, Bundy must have believed he could do anything he wanted to do, whenever and wherever he wanted to do it. And once again, he was correct.

Now that we know that Bundy was quite busy that first month, I'm going to address a subject that I've tackled (inconclusively, I might add, until now) in my second Bundy book titled, *The Trail of Ted Bundy: Digging Up the Untold Stories*. I'll be presenting some facts that I believe will put to rest a myth that's circulated among Bundy aficionados for a very long time. And this I will address in my next chapter.

DID TED BUNDY KNOW LAURA ANN AIME?

I first became aware of this supposed association when I was doing research for *The Bundy Murders*, and while I found the following stories in the official record, I must admit I had "problems" with it from the start. It's not that I closed my mind to the idea that what these people were saying was true; on the contrary, I looked for every reason possible to believe them, but that never occurred. As such, I never mentioned this scenario in my book. However, when I wrote my first companion volume, *The Trail of Ted Bundy: Digging Up the Untold Stories*, published seven years later, I made sure to include it because of how much debate I'd listened to from folks over the years. As such, I will be presenting some of what I wrote in that book which will give you a firm foundation of why I've finally come to my definite conclusion that the story has no real basis in fact, based on my recent understanding as to Bundy's hunting pattern that first month there. Let me also state, I don't believe that anyone is lying, or intentionally not telling the truth, and towards the end of this brief chapter I'll give my opinion as to why I do not believe Ted Bundy knew Laura Ann Aime prior to his abducting her.

What follows is from *The Trail of Ted Bundy*…

Another interesting back story to a Utah murder is related to the killing of Laura Aime. When I wrote The Bundy Murders, I stuck to the story that Bundy did not know Aime prior to her death, and this in fact may be the case (Bundy told *Florida detectives that he never harmed anyone that he knew). That said, these stories have circulated in some of the Bundy books, and so I will reproduce from the record that which has been told by some who knew Aime. What follows is again taken from the Colorado court document titled "Offer of Proof of Similar Transactions":*

"There will be testimony that Theodore Robert Bundy knew Laura Ann Aime and they had talked on several occasions. Witnesses will testify that Ted Bundy hung around Brown's Café, which was frequented also by Laura Ann Aime. Bundy drank coffee and flirted with the girls. Ted Bundy occasionally sat with Laura Ann Aime and her girlfriends. On one occasion when Laura Ann Aime was about to leave, Ted Bundy blocked her in a booth and stated 'You can't go, I'm going to rape you'; a witness to that, (sic) will testify that Laura Ann Aime shoved him out of the booth and left. This occurred in late summer or early fall of 1974. On another occasion, in late September or early October, Laura Ann Aime introduced Ted Bundy to a group of her friends, including Jim Stone (a pseudonym). Jim Stone and Ted Bundy got into an argument after Jim puts grass in Laura's halter top. Bundy told Jim to leave Laura alone because Laura was his girl. Laura told Bundy to 'get screwed.' Bundy was left speechless."

This does make for interesting reading, to be sure. But if you've read my first book on Ted Bundy, you know it didn't make the cut. It's not that I think this story can't be true, because it may very well be true. But it did not feel right to me the first few times I read it in 2007, and it doesn't feel good now. In other words, there's a big question mark hanging over it all, and it is for this reason I have left it out entirely the first time around. Still, it's interesting to contemplate.

Now, when I wrote these words in 2015, I was already well aware of a number of detractors in law enforcement who were never on board with the claim that Bundy knew

Laura Aime (although some were) prior to the murder, and they felt the above rendition of events just didn't add up. And in the years since, I've not only heard of more detractors who were players in the case, but on the flip side, I haven't heard even one thing that would cause me to believe it might be true. Even so, it's an interesting story, and some of the odd things they said Bundy said, I could certainly see him saying them. But that alone does not make these allegations true.

So, contemplating the above information, let's look at Bundy's life that September of 1974, and, might I add for our Laura Aime connection, much is now known about it by way of the recent information I've received from those who had interactions with the killer that month; activities that would preclude such a relationship forming in a small community so far south of Salt Lake City during that busy month for Bundy. And with this "preface", let us begin:

Bundy arrived in Salt Lake City in the wee hours of the morning of September 3, 1974. The night before he had picked up and murdered the unknown Idaho hitchhiker (he confessed to this at the end of his life), and then in the middle of the month, he flew home to Seattle and started packing an older model truck he'd purchased so he could bring the heavier things to his new apartment at 565 First Avenue. This apartment, which is very close to the University of Utah law school where he was enrolled as a first-year law student, was chosen for him by Liz on one of her trips back home to see her family. Bundy was so thrilled with the place, that as soon as he arrived, which was likely around 4 or 5:00 a.m., he telephoned Liz and told her how much he loved the place.

So far, we have at least the first three days that are a complete "wash" because of his travel time getting to Utah, and then at least two days (if not three) must be subtracted due to his moving of furniture from Seattle to Salt Lake City, etc. and as such, we have at least five days if not six where

Bundy couldn't have met new people even if he wanted to. Bundy's brother Glenn accompanied him to Utah to help him get everything up to his second-floor apartment, and perhaps as early as the next day (it is unknown by this author his exact date of departure), he caught a flight back to Seattle. And so, we have a very busy Bundy the first half of the month with his initial move, his return home, his getting his apartment in the kind of shape he wanted it (that alone takes time beyond the initial move), as well as any possible interactions he had with the law school during this time. I say during this time, because it appears that Bundy spent only three or so days in school that first semester, so we can't say for sure if he was even there in September, though I suspect he did at least make contact soon after his arrival.

Now, on top of all of this, we have the testimonies of Susan Milner, the newly-married young woman who encountered Bundy as she sat on a schoolyard swing while he was trying to entice her to take a ride with him in his VW (This story was published in my latest book, *The Enigma of Ted Bundy*), but the newly-married Susan refused. Susan also pegs this event very close to her wedding date which occurred in the Temple in Salt Lake on September 10th; that is, likely within two or so weeks. And now for this book, we have the valid contact interactions of Frieda Aid and Mary Christensen, who encountered Ted Bundy after he rang their doorbell of their first-floor apartment looking for that woman Bundy claimed was, like himself, a law school student at the university. Both incidents appear to have happened anywhere from mid-September to the later portion of the month; perhaps even very early October; or, as Frieda Aid said, "before the October murders". And here's what Susan Milner said, taken from my aforementioned book: *I don't remember exactly what month it was. It was very early into our marriage. I was pregnant but not showing yet, so I'm thinking the very end of September or early October of 1974.*

These late in the month or early October encounters make sense, as by this time Bundy was starting to feel well-settled in and most of the logistical things (filling his apartment and initial introduction to school), had been completed, allowing him more of the free time he needed to indulge his dark appetite for murder. Indeed, we can see similar circumstances after Bundy's escape from Colorado and his eventual arrival in Tallahassee. It appears that from the time Bundy fled from the jail in Glenwood Springs, Colorado, on December 30, 1977 until his attack on Chi Omega in the early morning hours of January 15, 1978, he not only didn't kill anyone, but that his desire to hunt again had only recently started to rise; and again, after he was settled into his rooming house on College Avenue once all the logistical stuff had been squared away, that dark, homicidal nature began to fill his mind once again, and two women and one young girl were going to die.

Now, let us return to what the documents state about Bundy supposedly frequenting Brown's Café, getting to know a number of people there, including Laura Aime, and even prior to the two above-mentioned events, both of which allegedly took place late September of early October. This time I will add commentary, in regular font and with brackets:

"There will be testimony that Theodore Robert Bundy knew Laura Ann Aime and they had talked on several occasions. Witnesses will testify that Ted Bundy hung around Brown's Café, (So, according to this, Bundy was hanging out on a regular basis at this obscure coffee house far away from where he lived at a time when he was known to be doing other things as described above. And just how early in September would Bundy have had to begin his regular sojourns south to make all these regular visits happen?) *which was frequented also by Laura Ann Aime.*

Bundy drank coffee and flirted with the girls. Ted Bundy occasionally sat with Laura Ann Aime and her girlfriends (again, note the frequency of Bundy's presence; so much so that "occasionally" during this regular visiting, he sat with Laura Aime). *On one occasion when Laura Ann Aime was about to leave, Ted Bundy blocked her in a booth and stated 'You can't go, I'm going to rape you'; a witness to that, (sic) will testify that Laura Ann Aime shoved him out of the booth and left. This occurred in late summer or early fall of 1974. On another occasion, in late September or early October, Laura Ann Aime introduced Ted Bundy to a group of her friends, including Jim Stone (a pseudonym). Jim Stone and Ted Bundy got into an argument after Jim puts grass in Laura's halter top. Bundy told Jim to leave Laura alone because Laura was his girl. Laura told Bundy to 'get screwed.' Bundy was left speechless."*

And so, what are we to believe about this tale of Bundy arriving in Salt Lake City, and almost "immediately" venturing south to tiny Lehi, Utah (population in 1970 was 4,659) so that he could "hang out" with the locals in such a nondescript place as Brown's Café; (in fact, "Brown's Café" was not the actual name, but a nickname for this establishment)? So again, we must ask ourselves: are we to believe Bundy arrived in the city and almost immediately started wandering down to a very small town where he decided that he should start spending a great deal of time there making "friends"? Could this even be possible? Well, perhaps in the sense that it's possible a meteorite might hit your house this evening, or that the lottery ticket you just purchased could bring millions of dollars into your life. But if we're to employ normal deductive reasoning and compare the allegations with those things we now know about Ted's comings and goings in the city that first month, then we must conclude that no, this story is absolutely not true; that is, it couldn't have been Bundy. There was just too much going on for this hungry killer to be going so far south and for so many days in the little town of Lehi.

In my view, I just don't see how it could have happened. And besides, Bundy's murderous genie was beginning to surface, and the last thing he would want to do is be hanging out in a small community and getting to know people, when he could be an "invisible" person hunting in a large city that would provide him with an enormous amount of "cover" as he sought out the women he wanted to kill. And now that we have two valid incidents showing Bundy was stalking victims in Salt Lake, his proverbial "backyard" if you will, it's clear his plans were to seek his prey in the heart of the city. And it would be foolish for us to believe these two known cases are the only women he approached in this particular area; no, there have to be others.

So, if this wasn't Ted Bundy, what caused this odd story to gain such traction over the years, putting Ted Bundy right in the middle of it? Well, I believe (and I'm not the only one) that this is probably a case of well-meaning misidentification on the part of those who were there. That is, there was a guy with dark hair and who drove a VW (one of the most popular cars of the 1960s and 1970s), who did in fact hang out at Brown's Café, who did in fact get to know Laura Ann Aime, and who did in fact spend a good deal of time in tiny Lehi, Utah.

And while in hindsight it's now clear that Ted Bundy neither had the time, nor the inclination, to do what some say he did during that September/early October of 1974, the authorities didn't have as clear a picture of his activities that month as we now do through revelations such as these. At the time this was going on, no one knew about Susan Milner's encounter with Bundy where he was clearly hunting, nor did they hear of Frieda Aid or Debbie Christianson who opened their door to find Bundy, as they would later learn, in the midst of his prowling. And because none of these women went to the police after Bundy was arrested and became a household name, investigators had very little knowledge of what he had been doing that month of September. And so, the stories from these folks claiming to know Bundy seemed plausible. And this is where, in my opinion, misidentification starts to make sense.

Of course, I understand some will continue to believe that Bundy arrived in Salt Lake City, a time in which he enrolled in school, flew back to Seattle for a short period to haul furniture back to Utah (his return trip in his truck can be tracked by his credit card gas purchases), and that he went to a tiny town almost 30 miles south of Salt Lake, apparently spent a good deal of time there, made friends, and was introduced to Laura Ann Aime. Given what we now know, I just do not see this as a possibility.

AN INCIDENT ON THE WASHINGTON STATE FERRY

It was my intention to finish the chapter about the Laura Ann Aime abduction and how it was impossible in my mind for Bundy to have met her in September of 1974. However, I recently received additional information about a possible Bundy incident that I, at this proverbial "last minute", have decided to add to the book. At the onset I must say that I don't know if the person described in this story is Bundy, and I'll correctly add there's no way of knowing if she had an actual brush with the killer. And yet, she may have. I say this because the story does contain some earmarks that may point to it being Bundy, and so because of this, I am adding the strange tale here. Outside of correcting some misspellings and typos, the message appears as I received it.

I want to mention as well that when you reach the point in her story where this person began being profane with her, she did not include the actual words that he said. When I asked her to provide them she did so. My point is, it's clear she was trying to avoid being graphic, but because we're talking about a possible Bundy encounter, I wanted to have all the known and remembered facts included in the story. And if this was Ted, then unlike his upcoming "rage" moment with the Utah probation and parole (see my book, *The Bundy Murders: A Comprehensive History*) that he was able to quickly bring under control, he didn't have to control anything here other that the volume of his voice.

Sara Barclay was born in 1955, and moved with her family to Washington State when she was a child. What follows is her communication to me via Facebook Messenger.

My birth name is Sara Barclay and I was born in 1955 in Missoula, Montana. I had a great Mom and Dad, and 3 siblings. We moved to Seattle when I was 2 and then we moved to a small farm outside of Issaquah, WA. in 1966. I had great and fairly typical childhood. It was of course a very interesting time to be transitioning from child to teen, and I went through the fairly normal teen rebellious times. I was in High (sic) school from '70 until graduation in 1973 when I was 18. I was extremely independent but had a good head on my shoulders, and started working in the restaurant business at age 17. My boyfriend was 20 yrs. old and had joined the Navy and ended up being stationed in Bremerton, Washington, which is where my story starts regarding my experience with Ted Bundy. I lived in a small mobile home right on Lake Sammamish near Issaquah from November of 1973 to March of 1974 and on my days off from work I would drive to the Seattle Ferry dock, board the ferry with my car, and then spend 2 days in Bremerton with my boyfriend. It was lots of fun and a new city and adventure for both myself and my boyfriend. One week during the winter I had some car problems, so instead of driving like usual, I had my friend Beth give me a ride to the Ferry Terminal, and I was a walk-on passenger. My boyfriend picked me up in Bremerton and after 2 days together he took me to the ferry terminal and I walked onto the ferry for the return trip to Seattle and would be calling my friend Beth (on a pay phone) to pick me up when I got back into Seattle. It was about a 2.5-hour trip around/across Puget Sound (Author's note: that trip by ferry today takes about an hour and 15 minutes to complete, and I don't know if this is a mistake of memory, or that travel time was longer then-as Sara will soon reference-because of stops the ferry would routinely make) *and I was just sitting down on the Ferry reading a book, and not paying any attention to anything or anybody. It was cold and stormy, and I was dirty and tired and ready to get back home. I do not know how long the man was standing behind my left shoulder, and he kind of startled me because I did not know he was there. He asked me what I was reading and I looked at him and then he came around nearer me and we just exchanged small talk, but I was actually kind of confused why this handsome, conservatively dressed (he was wearing a full suit and tie) man was talking to me. He was not being flirty at all... very polite, respectful, pretty normal acting. He introduced himself as Robert (I never forgot the name afterward) no last name. I felt pretty at ease but I thought it was strange that he was talking to me. I hadn't showered, no makeup, messy hair, and wearing dirty clothes, from hanging out at the beach for 2 days; and I had never had a man like him just start up a random conversation. There were some pretty big differences between the classes of people in the late 60's and early 70's and they didn't always cross those lines like nowadays. We talked a little about the book I was reading and he made small talk and asked me where I was coming from, going to, etc. I then decided that maybe he was trying to pick me up or something, so I made it really clear that I had been with my boyfriend so he would know that I had zero interest in him. He told me that he liked to take the Ferry from the South Puget Sound area because that way he could avoid all the bad traffic and long commute from there to Seattle. I think he said he worked either in Tacoma or Olympia in some sort of a state job possibly. That Ferry did stop at different locations so that was not unusual. "Robert" had fairly dark brown hair with a little wave in it, was about med length, not short, but not long either, brown eyes I think, a bit of a pointed nose, and it might sound funny but he had kind of slightly chubby cheeks. I am only 5 feet tall and he seemed to be fairly tall, standing next to me, so .... about 5-9 or 6 ft maybe. He was wearing a light brown or tan suit, possibly corduroy. It came up in the conversation that I lived in Issaquah (1/2 hour approx. from Seattle) and that my friend was picking me up. This whole time I would still be reading my book and really trying to ignore him, but I also did not want to be rude. He then asked me if he could sit down, and gestured across from me. I had been sitting on a wood-type old-style bench and he then sat down across from me, not super close, but within talking distance, on another bench. He then very nicely asked to give me a ride home, but that is when I started to feel uncomfortable. I guess looking back on it, I was young and still naive in many ways. I had thought I was so grown up at 18, and was so free and independent. I was not naive or had been sheltered though. I had been around many kinds of people, partied, drank, smoked pot, typical teenage stuff but I never was in trouble and had a pretty good head on my shoulders, was pretty careful and did not take very many risks. I had taken a self-defense class in high school and had learned quite a bit on how to protect myself. My mind now snapped to attention, and I realized that although he looked safe and pretty normal, maybe he thought I was a loose girl or something, and I did start to get a little concerned. I told him no thanks, that I already had a ride. He continued to stay nice and calm at this point, and said that he had no plans after the Ferry docked, he liked to drive, and that that way I would not have to bother my friend for a ride. I repeated no thanks (I have to admit that it was slightly tempting though). He did seem generally nice and harmless, but I had been taught like every other kid in America, to never get in a car with a stranger. I was not a hippie, maybe a little bit of a hippie wanna-be, but I did not hitchhike and was a pretty responsible working person. Ok.... Now is when the whole situation changed! He completely changed. He seemed to realize that he was defeated or I do not know what happened with him, but he changed... a lot. It very much surprised me. It shocked me. I was confused and definitely became alarmed. His face changed. His demeanor changed. His body language changed. He started talking to me almost as if he known me for some time, and just quickly throwing out questions at me. Why won't I take a ride with him? "Instead of a ride, would I like to come to his apartment with him? "It is in the U-District and not very far from the Ferry terminal". (I knew perfectly well where the U-district/North Seattle was) "Do you like waterbeds? "I have a nice, big waterbed!" He got weirder and madder, and his face was contorting and red. He was not really yelling or loud enough to cause a scene, but his voice was raising. He then turned vile and was using foul language. So excuse me but I will repeat what he said. "Do you like to fuck your boyfriend?" Do you want to come suck and fuck me on my waterbed? Have you ever fucked on a waterbed!? I can make you scream" or something like that. This all happened very fast, and as he was saying it I at first mumbled No or shook my head, and was busy now gathering up my bags, purse, book etc., and getting the heck away from this crazy guy. I felt very alone and scared of what he might try to do to me. The way he was acting I was now afraid he was so unhinged that he might try to hit me or grab me forcibly. The ferry was fairly full, but where I had been sitting was away from most of the other passengers, so it was quiet for reading. Now I suddenly remembered a story that I had heard (urban legend I think) that there were bad men that would get close to girls/women and inject them with a hypodermic needle of some sort of disabling tranquilizer or drug and kind of walking them to their car. This is what I thought he might try to do to me, and I remembered in my self-defense class that they told us if we got into a bad or dangerous situation with a stranger, to get away from them and try to interject yourself with families with kids or groups of people that can help and protect you if necessary. This is what I did. By now the Ferry was landing and people were all disembarking down the stairs to the lower level of the ferry ... either on foot (like me) or to their vehicles and would drive off. I never looked back or saw where "Robert" went. I never saw what kind of car he was driving. I was definitely worried that he could be trying to follow me or was watching me, but it was crowded and I just stayed next to the Ferry ticket office and called my friend on the pay phone to come pick me up. She came within about 1/2 hour and I was very freaked out on the phone and when I was in the car with her. We discussed calling the police, but agreed that we just wanted to get away from Seattle as soon as possible and that I did not have that much of a reason to call them. He never hurt me, and the police couldn't do anything about what had happened. This all happened months before we heard about the kidnappings and "Ted", so there was not the type of hysteria that came later. I am just writing this as I remember it. I have never forgotten it, learned from that experience, and I was always much more careful after that scary interaction. To the best of my knowledge, and from looking at a calendar of that time frame, narrowing it down by the weather and that my boyfriend broke up on my birthday March 4th 1974, that this happened sometime between December 1973 and February 1974. I do remember being surprised that there was some snow and ice on my driveway, when my friend drove me home to Issaquah and that I was a little surprised as that is a little later than normal for Issaquah Valley area. I was dealing with a lot of fear, and adrenaline and maybe that is why somehow my mind remembered so much of what happened and the weather that evening. Thank you for listening and forgive my writing and punctuation skills. I absolutely did not know that "Robert" was Ted Bundy until later, which I can explain to you, and you can ask me anything or about any other details I might have missed here. I did want my story to be documented somehow, but I also was not abducted or hurt by him, and just a very scary encounter with him. I do not know if he had already killed anybody before or around the time this happened, but I really do think it happened in February 1974, possibly earlier, but not later than Feb. You had mentioned to me before that he may have been honing his skills and learning from his mistakes. I feel so very terrible and sad for all of his victims. I do not know a ton about him, but I know he was very evil. If by your researching and writing about him you can possibly help and prevent future serial killers or give readers information to keep them from falling victim, that is a very good thing. I guess I have been very interested in learning if there was ever any info about him using the Washington State Ferry system, and if there were ever any missing girls or woman who rode the ferry around the time I did, or even around the waterfront area near the terminal. Sorry, this is so long. I am a pretty normal 66-year-old woman that is living my best life here on the Oregon Coast, and I really appreciate you taking the time to listen to me. I probably missed something, so just ask me anything you like. Thanks.*

It is interesting to note the man's reddened and contorted face when confronted with Sara's rejection of his offer to give her a ride home, or his switch to come to his university district apartment. Responding to her in that manner is not unlike something Bundy would do; or, more appropriately, something that could suddenly erupt out of Bundy if the person across from him happened to say the "wrong" thing, setting him off. During Bundy's pre-sentence investigation after his conviction for abducting Carol DaRonch, immediately after the probation and parole officer asked Ted about his real father, Bundy's face became reddened and contorted, but at this moment at least, he was able to quickly pull his rage back within himself. If this person

Sara encountered was Ted Bundy, her rejection of him (perhaps Bundy believed she would be an easy mark?) set him off to where he at least could show his anger with profane utterings, but do so in a way not to draw attention from those nearby.

Again, we can't say who this individual was, and it's unlikely we'll ever know; unless, of course, it was Bundy and he later mentioned it to someone like Bill Hagmaier, or one of any number of folks he interacted with over the years. Secrets can still rise to the surface.

I was recently told of two times Bundy used the ferries in the area and these are confirmed, but it's likely his use of the ferries exceeded this number. The same goes with cars Bundy used in abductions or attempted abductions that occurred either before he purchased his infamous beige, 1968 VW Bug, or afterward. Bundy used other vehicles more than many people realize.

MIKE MCCANN

Because I've mentioned Mike McCann several times in this book, as well as referring to him in a couple of my previous Bundy books as a "fellow Bundy researcher", or something along those lines, I think it's appropriate I mention how we came to know each other and became friends.

In 2010, I received a phone call from a fellow by the name of Mike McCann. Mike, it turned out, had a great interest in the Ted Bundy case, and as he would explain over the phone, his uncle had once dated Bundy victim, Georgann Hawkins. Mike mentioned he'd read my book, *The Bundy Murders*, published a year earlier, and said he was researching the case himself; even mentioning he was working on a documentary about Bundy. I could tell the fervor for the case was absolutely a part of his life.

Because Mike knew I had a lot of Bundy case file material, he asked if I would copy and mail them to him (all of this at his expense, of course). However, because he'd already mentioned he lives in Tacoma (and only, as I found out later, a few minutes' drive from his house to Bundy's boyhood home at 658 N. Skyline Drive), I suggested he contact Janette Gomes at the King County Archives in Seattle, and assured him she'll be happy to assist him in obtaining any files he needs. Not only that, but I asked if he'd been in contact with retired King County detective, Bob Keppel (the lead investigator for the Bundy case in Washington State), and he said no. I then encouraged him to get in touch with Bob as Bob had been very gracious to work with me during the research for my book, and I was confident he'd do the same for Mike. Well, Mike did reach out to Bob Keppel and they became and remained friends until Keppel's death in 2021. And later, Mike asked me if I would contact retired Bundy case detectives Jerry Thompson of Utah (now deceased) and Michael Fisher of Colorado, to see if they'd work with him. I did so and both men agreed.

Mike would go on to reach out to others who'd played important roles in the Bundy case, and because we occasionally talked by phone (it always pertained to Bundy), he'd tell me some of the discoveries he'd made along the way. And because I too decided to write additional books about the killer, I would spill some on my "secrets" as well. And of course, we humorously kept saying to each other, "Don't tell anyone about this!" followed by the oft-repeated promises that we wouldn't say a word.

Now, I should add that I've had a good number of people reach out to me for advice, saying they too were working on Bundy projects. As such, I've fielded a lot of questions about Bundy and the case to such folks over the years. And whenever this occurred, I answered each and every request for information to the best of my ability. And of all those who've connected with me, only three, to my knowledge, have followed through to a conclusion on their respective projects; and of the three, only Mike McCann has exceeded my wildest expectations.

Not only was Mike the guy behind the 2012 documentary, *Ted Bundy: The Death Row Tapes*, but he also was the man behind the *Amazon* documentary, *Ted Bundy: Falling for a Killer*. Not only that, but he obtained from Bundy's girlfriend, Liz, Bundy's DNA that was retrieved from a stamp on a letter sent to her by Ted, and after having it tested, McCann was able to debunk that persistent myth that Bundy's Grandfather, Samuel Cowell, was his father. I never put a lot of stock in this wild claim, mind you, but finally getting to the truth was gratifying. I must also add that Mike has a book coming out in the near future, and he's made some interesting discoveries over the years. And it's a book I look very forward to reading, and adding it to my Bundy collection of books.

THE TRANSCRIPT OF THE BIOGRAPHICAL MEMORIAL OF KATHY PARKS

Those of you who've followed me in my many years of researching and writing about Bundy, know very well my sincere desire to bring out everything possible pertaining to the victims in every book I've written; and this is something readers have certainly noticed. For *Ted Bundy's Murderous Mysteries,* I again took a greater look at a number of the women Bundy murdered, and this included Kathy Parks. Now, as to this biographical memorial, I have mentioned it in two of my previous books, and I published the small introduction only to this in-depth and personal document in my book, *The Bundy Secrets.* The memorial itself is both long and detailed, comprising 34 single-spaced pages. And what makes this worthwhile reading is that its author, Charles Parks Sr., is Kathy's grandfather; a grieving grandfather, I might add, yet he found it important to create this fine memorial to his granddaughter.

Not only this, but the memorial was completed in October 1975, just as Bundy was about to become a serious suspect in the case. Most of what you read pertaining to the case of the missing and murdered women will be correct, and where it's not (because of what authorities later learned), I will correct by way of "Author's note". Finally, I have decided to reproduce the entire the document (*Author's note: minus the last four or five pages that are not relevant to the Parks abduction, as the author cites other cases, etc.*) as Mr. Parks gave the King County Police a copy of the memorial, apparently desiring it to become a part of the case material. However, for those wanting to obtain an actual copy from the archives, it can be located in the Ted Bundy case collection at the King County Archives in Seattle, Washington. Reference number for this document is box 34, folder 13.

KATHY

A Biographical Memorial

1954 – 1974
By
Charles E. Parks

I. FORWORD (sic)

This is a biographical memorial of my granddaughter Kathy Parks, second daughter of my son, Charles E. Parks, Jr, and his wife, Katherine.

You will find it somewhat different from the customary memorial of this nature. It incorporates the latest chapter of the Parks Family History, which describes in some detail Kathy's abduction, the investigation of her disappearance, the discovery of her remains, and the final acts in the tragedy.

It then gives a brief biography of Kathy, tells of incidents in her life I am familiar with, and then gives an analysis of her character. This character analysis is based largely on an analysis of her relations with her immediate family and others, and on certain letters and notes she wrote reproduced here. After reading these letters, I realized that I did not really know my granddaughter during her lifetime. You, too, will have a better understanding and truer picture of the kind of girl she was and the kind of woman she hoped to be after reading them.

Because of its very personal nature, the text is often presented in the first person and addressed to the reader in the second person. My relationship with Kathy and with many readers makes this possible.

To visualize Kathy as she really was, the portfolio of pictures depicting her at all ages and her brief and tragic life is not included in this memorial. However, the portfolio will be found in the Parks Family History to which all members have access.

Charles E. Parks
October 1975
Orchid Springs
Winter Haven, Florida

II. THE ABDUCTION

The year 1974 marked the most tragic occurrence in the history of the Parks family—my granddaughter, Kathy, daughter of Chas. Jr. and his wife Katherine of Lafayette, Cal., was abducted from the campus of Oregon State University in Corvallis, Oregon, where she was a student. Ten months later some bones of her mutilated body were found in a woods near Seattle, Washington. She could be identified only from her dental records.

With Kathy's remains were found the bones of three other young women who disappeared about the time Kathy did and under similar circumstances. Two other skeletal remains had been found a few months previous about five miles from the site where Kathy's remains were found.

The finding of these remains marked the end of an organized search on the West Coast for the missing girls, all of whom were college students and disappeared under similar mysterious circumstances. At first it was believed they had left their schools voluntarily, as so many girls of their generation have done and that they would soon reappear, but as days, weeks and months went by with no indication of what had befallen them, it gradually was assumed they had been kidnapped or had met with foul play. A more intimate knowledge of the character and lives of the girls caused many to believe they had been abducted and murdered.

When Kathy's remains were found, it marked almost one year of wondering and worry on the part of her family and friends, as well as bafflement on the part of the police as to what had happened to her. There were absolutely no clues, only implications and theories, but no real facts on which to base a theory.

All that is known is that Kathy was last seen on May 6, 1974, leaving her campus residence alone about 11:00 p.m. after telling her friends that she was going to the student union four blocks way for an ice cream sundae. She had done this often before.

The same day she had learned that her father had suffered a massive heart attack. For a time it was believed she was so upset by this news that she had walked to the highway and impulsively decided to hitch a ride home. Her absence from her room was not even noted for two days. (*Author's note: Kathy had promised Lorraine Fargo, whom she met and spoke with on the sidewalk right before entering the Memorial Union Commons cafeteria, that she would come back in a little while and the two would continue their conversation. However, when Lorraine had not heard from Kathy by 2:00 a.m., it bothered her and she felt something could be wrong. And by the next morning, when others learned she never returned from her walk, people began searching for her and the authorities were alerted.*)

Chas. Jr.'s heart attack and Kathy missing put a great strain on the family and especially on her mother, who was warned not to disclose to her husband the fact that Kathy was missing. As a result, she was forced to sit in a hospital room watching her husband, who might be dying, and yet unable to tell him that his daughter had disappeared. All of us shared her agony. When the doctor finally permitted her to discuss Kathy's disappearance by telling her Chas. Jr. is out of danger, we all felt a sense of relief, but our relief did not lessen our anxiety over Kathy's disappearance.

The security force of the University and the police department of Corvallis made a minute investigation of Kathy's movements on the days preceding her disappearance. They found evidence she was disturbed emotionally-for example a letter written to her boyfriend attempting to break off their relationship but never mailed was found in the waste basket (sic) of her room. He had been urging her to leave school and move to Louisiana where he was working.

Her immediate friends felt she was also dissatisfied at school. Before leaving for the student union on the night of her disappearance, Kathy rebuffed their efforts to "talk it out" as they sensed she was disturbed. A schoolmate from Lafayette, even urged her to return to her room and discuss her problems to get a right perspective but Kathy refused.

Because of these early developments, I never believed Kathy had been abducted. I believed the pressure on her had become so great she had simply decided to disappear for a time and that her father's heart attack triggered her action. I believed it was only a question of time and she would resurface and discounted the fact that she had left all her clothes behind as well as her cosmetics and small sum in her bank account. Also, hundreds of girls were disappearing each year and they usually reappeared after a few days or a few months, so I was not particularly worried about Kathy surfacing, although much concerned about the effects of her experiences while she was away. Because of her nature, I wondered if she could take it. She was not the type that could take life's privations.

While no actual clues were found as to Kathy's fate, certain facts developed that lead some authorities to believe she had met with foul play. Within a period of four months before Kathy's disappearance, three other young women of her age had disappeared from campuses in Washington under very similar circumstances and two had disappeared from a Washington State park. In addition, two young hitchhiking girls 14 years of age had been found with their throats cut.

A University of Washington coed, Lynda Ann Healy, disappeared on January 31st from her apartment. (*Author's note: Bundy actually entered her basement apartment in the early morning hours of February 1, 1974.*) Blood was found in her room and the police suspected foul play. Her apartment was shared with four other girls but they heard nothing during the night. (*Author's note: for those unaware, Lynda lived in a two-story house with bedrooms throughout, including the basement where the owners had partitioned a section of it making it two bedrooms, one of which was Lynda Ann Healy's.*)

Donna Gail Manson, 19, a freshman at Evergreen State College near Olympia, Washington, was last reported seen at two p.m., March 12, when she left her dormitory for a jazz concert on the campus. (*Author's note: that concert was on the first floor of the library, and Donna did not leave her dormitory for first year students, until a few minutes past 7:00 p.m. Her walk would have placed her almost immediately on a path through the campus that was encased in trees (as many of them are), and there are no reports of anyone seeing her after she left her dorm.*)

Susan Elaine Rancourt, 18, a freshman at Central Washington State College at Ellensburg, was last seen leaving a meeting on the campus at ten p.m., April 17, walking towards her dormitory. The next morning her clothing was still in the washing machine.

Georgann Hawkins, 18, a student at the University of Washington, was last reported seen at one a.m. on June 11, walking toward a well-lighted passage way (sic) to a sorority house less than 100 yards from her destination. She vanished before she reached her living quarters. Through witnesses, police have traced her to within 20 feet of her destination. *(Author's note: after Georgann's disappearance, there were statements from witnesses that a man hobbling on crutches and carrying a briefcase, was walking along 17th Street N.E (Greek row comprising sorority and fraternity houses) and appeared to be in need of help; and received said help from at least one woman who carried his briefcase as he was crossing the street. Later, Ted Bundy would "confess" in the third-person concerning what had happened that night. And at the end of his life, he confided to Detective Robert Keppel, that he encountered Georgann in the alleyway and convinced her to help him carry his briefcase to his car one block away, whereupon, he knocked her unconscious, placed her in his car, and murdered her soon after. When Keppel asked him if there was anything that he could tell them about this abduction that only police and he would know, Bundy said that Georgann had lost the button to her pants and was keeping them secured with a safety pin. Upon hearing this, Keppel knew beyond a doubt that Ted Bundy was her killer.)*

Authorities tried to find a connection between the disappearance of Kathy and these four girls. Also, dozens of leads were reported as a result of intensive searches for all five of the girls, but they led nowhere.

All the victims were typical American college girls between 18 and 21, intelligent and well-liked. All wore their hair long and were pretty. Each girl disappeared at night between 9:30 p.m. and 1:00 a.m. from their college campus located near a state highway. None had announced any intentions of leaving and had taken no clothes or personal belongings.

III. THE SEARCH FOR KATHY

When informed of Kathy's disappearance I immediately offered a reward of $500 just for information that would lead to her whereabouts on the assumption that would bring some leads if she had voluntarily run away. Simmons Company offered an additional $1000. In addition, we contacted a lawyer, Todd Brown, who lived in Corvallis, a friend of Dianne's from Cedar Rapids, and asked him to keep in touch with the situation and report to Chas. Jr., who was beginning to be upset because of the lack of results being obtained. He went to Corvallis as soon as the doctors permitted and there met Bill Harris, a young criminal investigator of the University, to whom he took a great liking and who was in charge of the investigation. He made frequent reports to Chas. Jr. that served the purpose.

A day or so after Kathy was reported missing, Paul Kaehler, her brother-in-law, went to Corvallis and spent a week working with the university security people there.

Kathy's boyfriend, Christy McPhee, also soon appeared on the scene from his home in Louisiana and offered to help. After being interrogated closely by the police, he was cleared and immediately began to assist in the search. He traveled all over on country roads and posted a circular showing a picture of Kathy and the offer of the $1,500 reward for information as to her whereabouts. This brought quite a number of leads but they all led nowhere and only consumed the time of the police and the security investigators.

Bill Harris personally called on all the "hippy" (sic) communes within a 100-mile radius of Corvallis in an attempt to locate Kathy. Surprisingly, he reported he was given assistance and information in his search at all the places he visited, but the leads he obtained also proved worthless.

Another search was conducted by the Benton County Department of Emergency Services engaged in by about 125 people. They combed most of the country by car, motorcycle, boat and on foot, but no trace was found of the missing Kathy. In addition to the Benton County people, member of Explorer Post 120, Mary Peak 4 Wheelers and the Sheriff's Posse participated; plus units from Lane and Linn Counties engaged in searches in both counties; plus individual volunteers-about 300 participants in all-but without results.

As a result of this investigation, and four weeks after Kathy disappeared, the authorities were completely baffled. Not a single piece of evidence was developed, and as one homicide lieutenant said, "At this point we couldn't arrest a suspect even if we had one."

Having developed no direct evidence, they began to resort to theories. The most pronounced was that someone connected to the college campuses was involved, since the girls were all coeds.

Another was that a male-female team was involved, because the girls would be more inclined to trust a female, enabling the team to abduct her more quietly and easily.

Then it was suggested that the girls may have been shanghaied into a life of prostitution in brothels overseas, an idea based on an article in one of the far-out periodicals.

All kinds of bizarre theories to account for the disappearance of the girls were advanced. One police caption even suggested they consult a psychic. The sheriff of another county said he believed the "Zodiac" killer, who is said to have murdered 40 women in four western states so their spirits can serve him in the hereafter, could be responsible. Suicide was ruled out because of the number of girls involved and the fact that no notes or bodies had been found.

IV. THE ONLY LEAD

Then in August, 1974, a possible lead occurred when investigating an attack on several girls on the Washington State campus involving a young man driving a yellow Volkswagen. There a student described to the police an encounter she had with a young man just four days after a fellow coed had disappeared. According to her, she observed a young man with an arm in the sling carrying some books which he dropped as he neared her. She offered to assist him and was told he was in pain. She picked up the books and accompanied the man for several blocks to the Volkswagen and placed them in his car. The man then invited the girl into his car but she refused. He then tried to force her into the vehicle but she broke away and ran for help, but he had driven away. (This attempted abduction occurred four days before Susan Rancourt disappeared from the same campus). (*Author's note: this is the attempted abduction of Jane Curtis from Central Washington State College, which occurred on Sunday evening, April 13, 1974. It is incorrect that Bundy tried to force her into the car and she did not need to "break away" from him. She was leery of Bundy but she was able to get away without an actual attack happening. For the story of this encounter, see my book, The Bundy Murders: A Comprehensive History, or read her complete transcript in my book, Ted Bundy's Murderous Mysteries: The Many Victims of America's Most Infamous Serial Killer.*)

The girl gave a good description of the man. He is described as about 25-years-old, brown curly hair, weighing 165 pounds, about 5' 7" tall and his left arm was in a sling. She also reported the car had no front passenger seat.

Another Central State College coed also reported a confrontation with a man under similar circumstances. A senior said she had left the library and was walking towards the parking lot when she heard books dropped behind her. She looked back and saw a young man who had his right arm in a sling trying to recover them. He asked her for help in carrying the books to his car, located in an alley in the parking lot. (*Author's note: it was not an alley, nor a parking lot. Bundy had actually parked in a no-parking area where there was a railroad trestle that was bounded by fairly tall grass. Not only this, but it was not well-lighted and was in fact, the most desolate area on the campus. Bundy obviously picked this location knowing that once an attack began-he no doubt had his short 17 ½ inch crowbar lying under the rear tire on the passenger side, as he had done with other abductions- he could strike her and render her unconscious, and no one would see them. And this exact scenario likely took place on Thursday, April 17th during the successful abduction of Susan Rancourt.*) She agreed. When they reached the car, which was a brown Volkswagen, he fumbled trying to open the car door and dropped the keys. He asked her to pick them up but she said, "I wasn't about to bend over in front of him and asked him to step back in order to see them." She spotted the keys, scooped them up, dropped them in his hand and quickly walked away. The man made no effort to stop her. The girl said that during the walk to the car the man seemed harmless enough although "kind of weird", just enough to make her a little suspicious. When she heard that Susan Rancourt had vanished about the same time, she reported the incident.

The first concrete evidence relating to Kathy's disappearance and the other four college girls was brought to light early in September, 1974, when the remains of two bodies, possibly three, were discovered near Lake Sammamish State Park in Washington by goose hunters. Only bones were found. Two of the bodies were identified by dental charts as Denise Naslund of Seattle and Janice Ott of Issaquah. Both young women vanished July 14 from the park, two miles from the site where the remains were uncovered. They were not college girls.

Ms. Ott was a probation officer for the King County Juvenile Court and was last seen leaving the park with a young man who had identified himself as "Ted". He wore a cast on one arm. (*Author's note: it was a sling, not a cast.*) Witnesses said Mrs. Ott agreed to go to the parking lot with him to help load a sailboat on his trailer. (*Author's note: actually, Janice Ott had agreed to go with Bundy to his "folks" place in Issaquah, where she would help him get the boat on a trailer and bring it to the lake to sail. She said she expected to meet his parents, and when she mentioned to Bundy she didn't know how to sail, he said it would be "easy to teach you".*) She was never seen again.

Miss Naslund, who apparently didn't know Mrs. Ott, vanished later that same afternoon after leaving friends to walk to a restroom.

The other body, which was only a leg bone and part of some vertebrae, could not be identified (*Author's note: we must keep in mind that this memorial was written shortly after the events, and as such, much was still unknown. However, Bundy would later confess that the third set of bones found in the Issaquah hills belonged to Georgann Hawkins. Bundy also told Washington State detective Bob Keppel, that Bundy admitted burying Georgann's head at a hillside around 50 yards from where the other remains were located. However, a search of the hillside turned up nothing. Did Bundy lie about this? I doubt it, which means*) *her skull remains a part of the Issaquah crime scene to this very day.*) All the bones were scattered over an area about 150 feet in diameter. Authorities assume this was done by coyotes. They could not determine how the girls died.

Later four other young women recalled they had been approached the same day by an affable young man who called himself "Ted" and wore one arm in a sling. He had asked each girl to help him put a sailboat on top of his car. One woman had walked with him to the brown Volkswagen but backed away when she could see no boat.

The finding of these bodies spurred the search for the five coeds, including Kathy and the four girls from the Washington colleges. The search centered on the mysterious "Ted", who was seen twice at the Washington State College, at Evergreen State College, and particularly at Lake Sammamish State Park where he was seen and talked to a half dozen people. They all gave a similar description of him. A composite drawing was made from the descriptions and was widely distributed. Bill Harris spent some time in King County looking for clues that would link the finding of the two girls' bodies with the disappearance with Kathy but without results.

V. THE DISCOVERY

On March 3, 1975, two young forestry students on a routine inspection trip in the dense forest in the vicinity of North Bend, Oregon (*Author's note: he should have written, North Bend, Washington, and the date was actually March 1st*), in the Taylor Mountain area, found a skull east of Highway 18. The next day further search resulted in finding a second skull, along with small bones and pieces of bones. As the search continued, a portion of a human leg and arm bone together with long strands brownish-blonde hair, were found. The site of these finds is about 10 miles east of Issaquah, where the remains of Janice Ott and Denise Naslund were found in September after vanishing from Sammamish State Park in July of 1974.

The first skull found was that of Brenda Carol Ball, 22, of Normandy Park, who disappeared on June 1, 1974. She was last seen in a tavern about two a.m. of that day.

As the search continued, other jaw bones and skeleton remains were found. These were identified through dental charts as Lynda Healy, Susan Rancourt, and Kathy. This left two of the girls who vanished from their campus to be found. No more bones were located although 200 men composed (sic) the search force that combed the area on their hands and knees in the dense woods for several days. Those included young Explorer Search and Rescue volunteers from as far away as Spokane and Dayton, the Civil Air Patrol, and units of the National Guard, plus more than a dozen search dogs and their handlers. There were no indications, according to the police, that the remains were only those of four persons. Nor could they discover from the remains how death could have occurred or where or how they died.

The finding of these bodies intensified the search for "Ted", whom police believe is involved in the death of at least eight young women who vanished in the states of Oregon and Washington.

When the remains of the girls were found, theories as to the motive and means of the murders bean to extend into the fantastic. Although it has not been established that the same man was responsible for all the deaths, one California sheriff believes only one man (is) responsible for these reasons: the murder of 14 California girls were similar; their bodies were all dumped like garbage along a highway; the victims all looked alike; they were all about the same age; they all wore their hair parted in the middle; they wore casual clothing and they all had pierced ears. Asked how it would be possible to select his victims according to specifications, he said he must have interviewed and inspected them before he abducted them! And his reason? He must first decide who are fitted to be his slaves in the after-life!

The promulgation of such a theory indicated the degree of frustration law enforcement officers had reached in trying to solve this case. Some of them openly suggested that as a last resort, a psychic be consulted. "I'm willing to try anything," said Herb Swindler, a veteran detective police captain who heads the Seattle Police department missing persons unit. "I lie awake nights thinking about these girls," he said. "I have a daughter too, you know."

"We're at a dead end," said Inspector Charlie Gralf of Thurston County. "We're up against a blank wall," echoed Officer Bill Harris of the Oregon State University security force in making a resume of his efforts to locate Kathy and her murderer.

Even when the four bodies were found and identified, this development resulted in no clues. Even the identification was difficult and made only from dental charts. There was no real evidence in the case whatsoever and the only clue was the mysterious "Ted" and his yellow Volkswagen; which was sometimes described as brown. Even the description of "Ted" was mixed up, some saying he was well dressed and had an English accent while others described his appearance as nondescript with shoulder length, unkempt hair-a hippy (sic).

With this scanty clue police of several counties and cities started all over again in an attempt to solve the most macabre murder in the history of the Northwest. A special taskforce of King County and Seattle police detectives was also formed to probe the disappearance of the girls and the subsequent death of four whose remains were found in the Taylor Mountain area, the two other young women and an unidentified third victim found east of Issaquah. Two other young women remain missing. This task force will operate entirely independent of the regular homicide unit and will start at the beginning when the first young woman disappeared.

Attempts to bring the F.B.I. into the case were unsuccessful at this writing, as it is claimed murder is a local problem and the F.B.I. is not authorized by law to make an investigation of a crime of this nature. The agency offered to render every assistance possible but it could not conduct an investigation. This decision was a severe disappointment to the Parks family as they contended that Kathy had first been kidnapped and carried across a state line from Oregon to Washington where her body was found, and kidnapping under such circumstances is a Federal offense.

Police believe the murderer is a native of the locality where the bodies were found as they were all located within a radius of 10 miles and in a locality difficult to locate and search. Even Kathy's body was transported 270 miles from where she was abducted to the site where her remains were found.

As of now (October 1975) no progress has been made in finding a clue that might lead to Kathy's murderer, but theories abound. One recently originally in Florida, where the bodies of nine young women have been found this year floating in canals or on the banks of waterways. The circumstances of each murder and the condition of the remains of each victim when found were all similar, which leads the investigators to believe they were all committed by one person. For example, in several instances the victim's car when found had one flat tire leading the authorities to assume that the murderer had flattened the tire and then offered to be a good Samaritan when the owner appeared.

The murder of these young women is so similar to those in California and Washington, and others in Utah and Colorado early in 1975 and the location pattern such that authorities believe there may be a connection and could mean that the murderer has worked his way across the country to Florida. But identification is handicapped by the fact that the murderer had no former contact with his victims until the time he killed them.

I had never accepted the fact that because Kathy was missing, she was dead, although her father and mother did so. But I began to have doubts when the bodies of Janice Ott and Denise Naslund were found and after ten months had elapsed since hearing from her. It was a distinct shock to realize that a girl like Kathy would be murdered. I simply could not bring myself to believe it.

The reason was Kathy herself and the type of girl she was. Why should anyone want to harm her, and even if one did, how could they go through with it to the point of snuffing out her life?

VI. THE TYPE OF GIRL THAT WAS KATHY

Roberta Kathleen Parks, the second daughter of Chas. E. Parks, Jr. and Katherine Parks, was born on February 27, 1954, at Lakewood, Ohio, a suburb of Cleveland.

If there is such a thing as an American race, Kathy was truly a member and an excellent example of what the "melting pot" is intended to produce. She can trace her lineage to no single national origin. While she represented the 15th generation of English in the United States and the fifth generation of Irish, she also had a direct line in ancestors of French, Dutch, Welsh, German, Swedes, Scandinavian and even Indian origin.

When born she was a premature baby and weighed only two pounds, nine ounces. However, she was a healthy baby although her mother at first despaired of her living long enough to even leave the hospital. The only indication of her premature birth was an elongated head caused by being forced to lie on her side. However, by the time she was four years of age, her features had assumed normal proportions.

We first became aware of Kathy when Chas. Jr. wired Connie for assistance in taking care of Sharon and her mother. Connie responded immediately and left for Cleveland. Kathy was born a few days after Connie arrived. I visited the family later that summer and found Kathy a beautiful, well-formed baby and not the "preemie" expected. She was a very quiet baby.

Chas. Jr. and his family soon moved to Columbus, Ohio, and Connie, and all the children and I visited twice while they lived there.

When Chas. Jr. was transferred to Chicago, his wife Katherine, located a beautiful home in Barrington where the children attended school. As Barrington was located only 200 miles from Cedar Rapids, different family members visited Barrington frequently, particularly as my brother-in-law, "Duke" Kittredge and his family also lived there. I celebrated my 70th birthday with a party at Chas. Jr. home.

My memory of little Kathy at that time is of a very quiet child, in sharp contrast to her sister, Sharon, who was what we described as a "firecracker" and one who could not remain quiet for any length of time. One time, seeing us drive up the driveway, Sharon, as was her custom, came running to meet us and dove head first into the open car window to welcome me. Unfortunately, she missed the opening and her forehead struck the top of the car, knocking her out. Little Kathy, on the other hand, waited demurely for us to come to her.

While she was a baby and still in her crib, Kathy developed a trait that really alarmed me. She formed the habit of resting on her hands and knees and striking her head against the headboard, not gently, but with a resounding crack that could be heard all over the house, and she kept it up for what seemed hours. However, her mother was not alarmed and said the doctor had told her this was a common practice of some children; but he gave no reasons for the baby's action. Mother Kathy had training as a nurse but I always had a feeling of apprehension when I heard the drumming of little Kathy's head against the headboard.

As a girl Kathy obtained her elementary education at Barrington and enjoyed herself with the usual activities little girls engage in and making girlhood friends. In 1966, when Kathy was 12 years of age, her father was transferred to the pacific coast area with headquarters in San Francisco. As usual, Chas. Jr. left it to Mother Kathy to find a home and, as usual, Mother Kathy came through in a big way, just as she had at Columbus and Barrington. This time the home was located on a high ridge in the town of Lafyette, west of Oakland, with a beautiful view overlooking the town and the highway leading to San Francisco. Chas. Jr. built an oval pool and patio on the grounds.

We visited the family frequently at Lafayette but the activities and energy of Kathy's two sisters, Sharon and Susie (who was now maturing fast), pushed into the background the quiet and introverted Kathy. But one or two incidents stand out in my memory. Sharon and Kathy liked to swim in the pool and they frequently did so, playing a game called "Marco Polo". I forget the rules of the game as all I remember was Sharon and Kathy, continually and without any rest, jumping out of the pool, running to the diving board and jumping back in, chasing each other. I timed them once and they repeated this performance for one hour without interruption and then dropped exhausted on the grass. One of the impressions I got of Kathy then was how beautifully proportioned her limbs and body were, and how surprised I was that a girl usually so quiet could become so animated-on a par with Sharon. I also contrasted her with the small mite of humanity I had first seen.

Kathy finished school in Layfette and then attended Diablo Valley Community College during 1972-73, commuting from her home. However, she wanted to change to a larger school and live in a dormitory. The activities of the Cedar Rapids Parks seemed to have an attraction for Kathy, maybe because there were so many of us, and some of her cousins were more her own age. As a result, she decided to explore the possibility of attending a college near us. During Easter vacation of 1973 she and Sharon drove their car from Layfette to Cedar Rapids to investigate a college in Iowa. They were disappointed with the college and decided to visit Barrington and renew old friendships with girls they had known in school. I believe the result of their contacts at that time was the worst disappointment of their lives up to then. One of the childhood friends acted as though she didn't know them; another opened the door a crack when they called and asked what they wanted. I don't believe any were cordial or put out the welcoming mat. The two girls were really shocked and hastened back to Cedar Rapids, leaving the following day for California. Kathy transferred to Oregon State University at Corvallis, Oregon for the year of 1973/74.

In college Kathy was not satisfied with her studies or with her progress. She felt she was being "snowed under" by too many reading assignments and was determined to not let that happen. She particularly disliked a class called "Critical Thinking", which she described as "Philosophy", saying in a letter to Connie and me "...this aspect of the field of philosophy doesn't interest me. For example, an hour was spent today in class discussing the differences between a sentence, a statement, and an explanation. It seems to me that too much emphasis is placed on concepts that seem trivial to me, and I'm not interested in this type of discussion." Education was showing its effects on Kathy.

Later she explained she was interested in ideas expressed by the great philosophers because it was a pleasant challenge to try to grasp their ideas, but she had no curiosity of discovering and comparing the technique of how they expressed them-of word building or the rhetoric involved so stressed by the Greek and Roman writers and orators. Her interest, she said then, was in ballet, foreign languages and even in "World's Religions". This was because she was primarily interested in people, as she well expressed it in this comment when she first saw her first nephew, the new son of her sister, Sharon. "I've gone completely over for Kristoffer Lee Kaehler, as has my mother. We're both nuts over him. I can't help thinking he is really someone special-and that is my honestly biased opinion! I wish you could meet him-he really is a fascinating little boy and I know you would fall for him just like I have. I've always had a soft spot in my heart for anyone or anything that is new in this world."

If Kathy had added, as she did often in letters: "...or who needs help or is deprived...", this sentence would summarize one of her basic characteristics-sympathy for the underdog. This trait may have been a real factor in her murder.

The question arises: What type of girl was Kathy? What were her aims in life? Had she lived long enough to know what she wanted?

Those who knew her had little difficulty in describing her as her real character was well recognized by her friends and schoolmates. As her friend and classmate, Joanne Stevens, said: "Kathy was a beautiful and sensitive young woman who continually radiated love and warmth and expressed real concern with the problems of her friends. I felt quite secure in my association with Kathy, well knowing that she understood me, would always listen to me and that to her there was no such thing as a backdoor relationship. I often thought and wondered how a person like Kathy, who at times felt so insecure and dissatisfied with herself could so generously and easily recognize the good in others. She was alert, aware and continually searching for life. I will always be thankful for the privilege of having known her."

But the best way to know Kathy is to let her analyze herself and discover her hopes, her desires and how she regarded and what she expected of life in her own words.

In her room after she was abducted was a paper that outlined in vivid detail her ideas of life and her plans for the future as she visualized it at the age of 20. This was written during her Easter vacation in 1974. It is copied verbatim below:

"Life Goals"

"To be as happy and as good a person as I can be. To learn about life through living-to better myself as time passes in any way I can. I want to learn through school all my life, and also through experiences outside the academic atmosphere, which I consider valuable learning experiences, **just** as important, if not more so, than "book" learning. I want to be at peace with myself and in harmony with others.

"Experiences I want to get into:

"All or any aspects of the field of art-any kind of dancing, painting, ceramics weaving, macrame, singing, silk screening, printing, etc., etc. Learn how to play flute, guitar, sitar, zither, harp, learn woodworking, stained glass artwork.

"Try mountain-climbing, back-packing, camping, hiking for days, sky-diving, scuba-diving. Cross-country skiing, billiards, give any sports a try.

"For a career:

"At this point in time I would like very much to get into a field of special education – 1) working with mentally retarded kids, physical therapy. Plan on getting into that in the near future, a few years from now after I put myself through school after a break of a year or two-Very important! I want my job to be a challenging hobby, not drudgery. In my job, I want to be working either out-of-doors (secretary would be horrible-I'm a clock-watcher), with younger children, be my own boss of sorts. I'd also like to get into working in some field of art, be it dancing, weaving, or whatever, -as a backup-some skill I can fall back on, or throw myself into if I wanted. I plan on taking school courses off and on 'till I die.

"I want to love, and be loved. I want to live in an area I consider beautiful. I want to work at a job with a certain satisfaction and enjoyment.

"Kids-Well, now-don't know. If I will have them, I'll wait until I feel good & ready. I like kids in general, and I always thought that if the time comes when I want them, I'd go all the way. I'd like to have one just for the experience of it, and then adopt the rest-all ages, all kinds of kids.

"I want to be happy, and make others happy-I just want to give myself as good a life as I can-the good with the bad.

"I want to travel; experience lifestyles different from my own, live in different societies; meet different people, all ages. I want to get into gardening-I love plants and watching them grow. I want to keep myself healthy, physically and mentally, gain more confidence in myself. I want to love the people. (sic) I find it most difficult to love. I would like to have happiness, energy (natural) serenity, and a strong sense of peaceful well-being well up inside me. I want to be happy with myself and completely accepting of myself. I want to love and learn through loving and living. I want to live to be a hundred years old; but I think

I'll be ready for death whenever the time comes for me."

On first reading this paper seems to express the hopes and dreams of an immature 20-year-old girl who had not yet experienced life. It also gives some insight into Kathy's nature – a desire to learn; to experience the better things of life and really enjoy them; and, (sic) make others happy. And, it does something else. It indicates the seriousness of Kathy's character – that her thoughts were not on boys, on dates or parties, but on her future. It shows she was too trustful of others and fails to take into account she would meet with hostility in life. The very fact that she would put her thoughts and aspirations on paper at the age of twenty indicated an aspect of her nature that few girls her age reveal. Coupled with later revelations, it gives an insight into the type of woman she would become.

One summer a year before this was written, and while we were visiting in Lafayette, Kathy sought me out and wanted to talk. This was the first time a granddaughter or grandson had ever done this but it is another indication of the seriousness of Kathy's character. As I look back and remember, the subject of our conversation was just about as revealed in this paper and she wanted my opinion of her views. My opinion at the time was that she was an idyllic dreamer based on a lack of knowledge of real life, but I did not say this to her. I remember asking her, "Kathy, how are you going to live while doing all of this? Who will support you while you are doing all this studying, all the traveling, this seeking for the good life?"

I blamed her lack of practical knowledge on the lack of practical training she was receiving, calling a "bread and butter" job a "challenge" and making plans for a house without building a foundation, or ignoring its financing and the emphasis placed on "I" and "Me" by her counselors and teachers.

But Kathy had ideas here too, mostly impractical, and the discussion developed into ways and means of getting the right kind of job, and what was the right kind of job. I don't think she agreed with my advice, but the following summer found her working as a waitress in a local restaurant-a practice followed by many college girls. She was somewhat embarrassed here as she asked us not to visit the place to watch her in action, which we kiddingly threatened to do. She should not have been so sensitive as her cousin, my daughter Phyllis who is very much like Kathy, had a similar job at a resort in Lake Geneva while attending Northwestern and urged all the family to visit her on the job. However, my reactions were similar to Kathy's and I did not go although other members of the family did. This incident is an example of Kathy's sensitiveness which she inherited from her father and myself, as I am fairly certain her father never paid the restaurant a visit while Kathy was on the job, just as I never visited the restaurant in Lake Geneva.

Her father offered Kathy similar advice as he was a practical business man and he knew how important it was for a young woman to be able to acquire a job or profession that would help her financially. After Kathy departed, he found the following letter he had written to her on her 20th birthday framed on the wall of her room. In commenting on it, he said; "I cannot imagine now why I did not realize then how important little touches like this were to a young, sensitive, maturing girl."

"My dearest 20 yr. old No. 2 daughter-

It sure doesn't seem like 20 years have gone by since I was looking at you in an incubator at Lakewood hospital in Cleveland.

"As you approach the halfway mark in college, I hope you are giving serious thought to courses leading to a degree of professionalism that will give you financial independence if you desire that throughout your life.

"In any event, all my love, good luck and study hard. Have some fun with the attached check or buy some shoes or a dress.

"Love Dad"

A closer reading of "Life Goals" also reveals that Kathy's goals were not all the vaporing's of a teenage nymph. She did give a lot of thought to the practical aspect of her future-to the type of career she wanted, which was in the field of special education, working with young children or the mentally retarded. She acquired this idea from her contact with a school for the mentally retarded in Lafayette when she accompanied one of her classmates who was a volunteer worker at the school.

This was an example of Kathy's whole attitude-sympathy for the under privileged-and it may have resulted directly in her death if the theory of "Ted" as the abductor is correct. As her father said: "If Kathy had been walking across the campus, and saw someone with his arm in a sling struggling with some packages, she wouldn't have waited for a request for help."

Kathy's paper also revealed she knew what she wanted, and it was not office work as I tried to convince her that was what she needed to get started and not working as a waitress or as a maid at a resort hotel. She simply was not suited for that kind of work even temporarily, but she rebelled at what she considered office drudgery and wanted none of it.

Kathy's "Goals" also reveal her as self-centered, but what young girl isn't. She wanted "to find herself" and had the courage to say so in writing and the intelligence to analyze her wants to the extent that her life experiences permitted.

VII. OTHER CHARACTER CLUES

Kathy's character was also revealed in even more detail in three other memoranda she left behind. One was a letter addressed to her father. Like most businessmen, Chas. Jr. left the rearing of his children to his wife. He had also been in the Army for five years during WW2, rising from enlisted man to Captain, and had acquired certain habits of command. He expected obedience from his children without argument and also without being trained to obey. Modern children are not reared in this manner, but Chas. Jr. was too occupied with the job of making a good living for his family to realize this. As a result he and a daughter of Kathy's temperament and aspirations clashed. That is what this letter is all about. (*Author's note: the following letter contains certain words in bold print, and these are true to Kathy's letter to her father.*)

"Dear Dad"

"I was touched by your letter to me, so I thought I'd like to sit down and write a letter to you-just for you.

"I know our relationship has been a stormy one through the years and I realize we've hurt each other many times -I regret this-but it sometimes seems to me it was inevitable in the sense that our personalities are so individual, we are bound to clash in our opinions in many subjects. This is not bad in itself-people will always differ in their ideas to **some** degree-it makes for a more interesting world! What I regret in **myself** is that for the longest time, while I could not or **would** not comprehend your views, I also could not accept you as you are for thinking that way-therein lies the tragedy in my mind about myself-the fact that I couldn't accept you for thinking the way you do.

'It may seem almost absurd to you, but I'd like to apologize for the many years I could not accept you. I've been feeling as though I've been outgrowing it for the past couple of years-it was a slow process, but an extremely healthy one, I know. Being away from you this short length of time has also greatly altered my perspective of family relationships. I'd like you to understand that, in the future, no matter how greatly or violently we may disagree on anything, I can honestly say that I've finally, **finally**, accepted the unique individual you are. It is a great relief for me to discover that any hostility I may have felt towards you when I was 14 or 15 has dissipated, though I am deeply sorry I have hurt you in the past. I can only think now it is an experience I (and you also) can learn from. Learning from all my experiences, no matter how sorrowful, troubling, or happy is something I like to incorporate into my life. I think now I have learned much from the past experiences with you. In the future, I would like to be more openly honest with you with anything I might have to say. Hell may break loose and the roof fly off the house, but I think at least we will get to know each other better. In any case, I would like to tell you I love you very much, Dad, no matter how often we may end up at odds! I think our family has got to be a little freer with emotions, too. If I'm angry, I tend to do better by myself if I shout it out, rather than bottle it up and let the anger gnaw out my insides. Same thing if I'm happy-just **can't** hold **that in**! Well, I could write pages on the whole subject, but I've got a class in 10 or 15 minutes so it'll just have to wait. I just wanted to tell you I love you, and I'm proud of **you too.**

"I would like to live up to the expectations you and Mom hold for me here in school. Times are, I really feel I've done my best, and times are, I feel

I haven't-it's up and down all the way. I'll be glad when this term is over, and I can take classes up my alley (philosophy, literature, art, dance, etc.). These science, math, and history classes really get me down, and bog me down at times. I'm just not in my element at all with (sic) in science and math. While I find the subjects interesting in a "factual" sense, I've always felt that in taking them, I'm just skimming the surface of an immense well of more detailed information. Someday, when I find the time, I'd like to really try and rekindle my interest in the sciences, and delve into them at a greater depth just to see how far I can go. Right now, though, I'll be glad just to get through them and complete my general education requirements.

"Well, Dad, got to run-and thank you for the cheque. I'm going to use it to continue my belly-dance classes! I've had more fun learning how, and I don't want to quit in midstream, so your cheque is greatly appreciated!

"Hi to Mom, and I'll see you soon. Take care.

"All my love,

Kathy

This letter is far more mature than "Life Goals". It reads as if Kathy had reached a development far greater than the average girl of twenty. Few girls her age could write such a letter to their father. It was frank, admitted past mistakes and prophesied more in the future; expressed sorrow that her opinions often clashed with his, but indicated nothing could be done about it because their personalities were so different. Then she began to search for the good in such a situation and found it, at least to her own satisfaction-their quarrels made life more interesting; they caused her to comprehend his views and even respect them, and she blamed herself for not understanding or even trying to understand her father in the past. She apologized for this and for any hostility she may have shown towards him, but not for her convictions. This called for a strong personality and an honest self-appraisement. She also expressed the belief that her changed attitude would make for better family relations, more honesty on both their parts, and expressed her deep love for her father.

This letter itself gives a better insight into Kathy's character than anything that could be said. Her father appreciated it and was quite happy in receiving it. To me it revealed a facet of Kathy's character that I was not familiar with-the strength of her convictions and the fact that the fledgling was growing wings. To a grandfather of two generations back, there was only one sour note-the fact that she was going to spend the check her father sent her on "belly-dance" classes. I wondered if her belly-dancing had not been an issue between her and her father and if she mentioned it merely in the spirit of bravado or to assert her independence of his guidance. If that was the purpose, I must confess it was not in accord with the general tone of her letter. But, if so, it was evidence of her honesty. I do not know the real reasons for her quarrels with her father, but I do not believe they were too serious.

The letter from her father that prompted Kathy to write him in this manner is reproduced below. It was written spontaneously and for no particular reason after a busy day at his office, but it reveals a great love for his daughter which Kathy recognized and responded to. He was greatly upset after her death as for some reason he got the idea from some cruel remark of one of her girlfriends that Kathy considered him the "enemy". A reading of Kathy's letter should have convinced him otherwise, and it did so. My son was a real father to his daughter and Kathy realized it.

My dearest Kathy-
"Just a little note written in the office after all have gone home.

"I've been reading your letters, sweetheart, and I'm very proud of you. The University is hard work, I know, but I also sense you are giving it your best. And that is all we ask.

"School should not be all work, however, and hopefully you are making new and interesting friends. From your letters it would seem that your horizons and outlook on many facets of living are broadening. That is good.

"We'll miss you very much at Thanksgiving. Paul and Sharon were here yesterday (Sunday) For dinner. We all talked about you at length.

"Here's a small check for $10 to do whatever you want with-preferably something you wanted or wished you could do but didn't think you could afford.

"Go ahead and call Mom from time to time. It does her a great deal of good to talk to you.

"Have a nice Thanksgiving, darling. We love you very much.

"Dad"

If he had any doubts on how his daughter regarded him, he had access to another note she had written. She handed it to him personally just as he was about to board a plane, with this notation on the envelope: "Daddy! Please don't read before seated and served on the plane. (I'm not Kidding!!)"

"Dear Daddy,

"This is a really sad situation! Seems like lately all I can do is express myself on paper. This is a pre-thank-you note for the wonderful time I know I'm going to have in Mexico. I'm writing to Mom, too, but especially to you. I think I've inherited my traveling blood from you- (knowing how much you love to travel)-because all of a sudden it seems like there are a million places to see and things to do just opening up to me. First of all, I want to thank my lucky stars I have you both for parents. Never have I had so much fun in one summer in my whole life (traveling to places, visiting friends, etc.), Mexico, now, is like the crowning touch! Well, Daddy, I just wanted to say thank you (from the bottom of my heart, and I mean that!). Even though you and I don't, and won't, see eye-to-eye on many things, I know I can always count on you as a father.

"Love, Kathy"

"(P.S. I just read this over and I'm thinking what a lot of sentimental mush! But then, maybe I'm just feeling sentimental.)"

The next letter reproduced here was addressed to Connie and me. She addressed Connie as "Aunt Connie" because she was not her grandmother in name although she was in fact as few children ever had a more concerned or helpful grandmother than Connie. This was proven by an incident showing the reaction of Kathy's sister, Sharon, when she visited us for some time in Cedar Rapids. Connie often wore a grandmother's bracelet which listed the names of eight grandchildren which always made the children happy. Sharon noticed the omission of herself and her two sisters being not represented on the bracelet. Connie explained she had been told they were not her grandchildren and they should not be recognized as such on the bracelet. Sharon felt let down and lost so she said she would call her "Grandma" anyway and not "Aunt Connie", which made Connie happy. When Sharon returned home she made three hearts with the names of Sharon, Kathy and Susie and sent to Connie who attached them on the bracelet. However, out of force of habit, they still call her "Aunt Connie".

Kathy's letter follows:

"April 11, 1974

"Dear Grandpa and Aunt Connie"

"Just a note to wish you both a Happy Easter, and hoping all your days bring you a note of joy and gladness! Do you like Huiku (sic)? I have loved prose and poetry for a long time, and huiku is a special, favorite kind of poetry to me-Spring is bursting out in all her glory here in Oregon (although the rain still insists on remaining!). My spirits soar high in the spring, and I'd like you to read this little poem I found in an old book of Japanese huiku I have. There are cherry tress all over this campus, and on beautiful spring days, this poem seems to me to capture the riotous spirit of nature around here:

"Now from cherry trees...
Millions of maidens
Flying
Fierce War-Lord
Sadaiye

"Spring lightheartedness is certainly contagious. I'm having a rather difficult time of it concentrating on school work. I must admit I have a very, very bad case of Spring Fever!

"Well, I just wanted to say a quick hello to both of you, and wish you a happy Easter (although I realize this will be somewhat belated). I hope you are both well and happy, and that you two are just as infatuated with the loveliness of Springtime as I am. My heart is so full of love for you two-don't ever forget that!

"I love and miss you-

"Kathy"

This beautifully worded letter is typical of Kathy when she was in a happy mood. It was written just two months before she was abducted and is an expression of the kind of person she really was. But for some reason which I cannot explain it aroused an ominous sensation when I read it. I had the feeling that Kathy was about to do something of which we disapproved and that she was bidding us good-bye. The concern was focused on the sentiment expressed in the last sentence and particularly the last phrase. I associated her emotional expression with rumors we had heard of her affair with Christy McPhee and that she intended to join him in Louisiana.

Although I had met this young man only once, I wholly disapproved of him and this brief meeting convinced me that a young man of his type and background was as unsuited to a girl like Kathy as she was to him. Yet he must have exerted some influence on her. He was the only "boyfriend" she ever had and always treated him with the casual kindness modern young people treat each other. I could discern no indication of affection towards him on Kathy's part during this meeting nor did she ever mention him in her letters to Connie and myself. I have the feeling that this was just another instance of Kathy's sympathy for the underdog temporarily overcoming her better judgment just as when she asked her mother to permit her to date a total stranger whom she had met working in a street repair gang in front of her home because "he looked beat" and found on conversing with him that he was lonesome. But this was Kathy!

My impressions were confirmed by the method this affair was terminated. During the few months preceding her abduction Kathy had received about fifty letters from Christie, all urging her to give up her plans for an education and join him in the type of life he was living as a diver and an oil well worker in Louisiana. The only inducement he offered was that "he wanted her". What a reason to give to persuade a young inexperienced girl to leave college and change the lifestyle and future promises of a girl like Kathy.

Kathy's final answer is found in these excerpts of a letter she wrote to Christy but never mailed. It was found in a waste basket (sic) in her room after she was abducted.

"I have been thinking seriously about this upcoming summer and my future. I want to live and work in California and not in Louisiana. To be completely honest I have decided I am not yet ready to settle down.

"There is something I must do to be completely happy and at ease with myself before I settle down. I must know I can go it alone. At this point I am insecure and more than a little unsure of my own ability to cope with the world by myself. I want to build up my confidence and faith in myself. After that is done I can think of settling down, knowing I am a better person for it.

"This decision is nothing against you. My feelings towards you have not changed but I have changed my plans for the future. I need more time to become my own person, I need to grow and feel worthy of myself."

Apparently Kathy was torn between her natural desire not to offend anyone and a firm conviction dictated by common sense as to her future. There was no question as to which course she would take but the conflict caused her to delay her decision as long as possible. In the end she did nothing. Anyone who has read her letters reproduced here will realize that this "do nothing" method of making a decision was typical of Kathy. She never had any intention of moving to Louisiana-of permitting a casual relationship to change her lifestyle-her life's aims as she called them-even if her decisions caused another person distress.

From this letter we must regard Kathy as a pathetically heroic figure willing and anxious to face life alone seeking help from no one although handicapped by natural positive but conflicting instincts such as the desire to do what was right for herself and undue sympathy and compassion for others. These conflicts placed her at a disadvantage in Life's battle which she sought. And she lost the first encounter, paying the penalty with her life.

Kathy was not spiritually oriented. She had no religious background for the simple reason that like a growing number of American youths, she had no religious training. She did know the difference between right and wrong but I doubt if she accepted the moral code as I know it or even as her father and mother know it. This background had an influence on Kathy's life. I doubt if she ever considered appealing for spiritual help. I doubt if it ever occurred to her that there was a creator or supreme being, not that this was a fault of her character as her character had not time to jell before she was called away. So we must accept her as she was-the product of her own limited life experiences and the times in which she was being reared.

VII. FINAL ACT IN THE TRAGEDY

The final act in the drama of Kathy's life was a memorial service held on March 14 in Lafayette at the Lutheran Church, with the Rev. J. E. Rommereim officiating. This was the church Kathy occasionally attended with her friend, Joanne Stevens. Also, a substantial memorial fund was subscribed and turned over to the Las Trampas School for the mentally retarded at Lafayette for which Kathy was sometimes a volunteer worker. Over two hundred contributed to the fund, including members of the Parks and Wilkes families; business associates of her father, especially the officers of Simmons Company, including the general manager of the Pacific Division, the Chairman of the Board, the present and former presidents of the company; Kathy's friends and their families. In addition, others contributed to their personal charities and many Catholic masses were offered. As a memorial to Kathy, a plaque has been mounted on a door inside the educational building of the school.

In his sermon the minister asked the question: "Here was a young woman in the prime of her life, with health, intelligence, education, personality, family and friends-with everything to look forward to-suddenly snatched from this life by a deranged maniac. The question is 'WHY'?"

After saying there was no simple answer, he asked God for a reason and then attempted to interpret God's reasons by quoting scripture. I understood him when he said Kathy's death fitted into the creator's design which called for faith to understand. All I know is what my senses perceive-the interruption of a young life that was just beginning, that had been nourished to that stage with so much effort and expense and that had so many reasons for living and no good reason for dying so young, but nevertheless did die-brutally murdered. From a human point of view, it doesn't make sense, but neither does crime of any sort. I can see why the human feels called upon to appeal to the spiritual for solace and an explanation of tragedies such as this. And, it is fortunate that so many find in this quarter the answer they are seeking, but no answer, regardless of the source, can bring such a lovely human being back to life as we knew it.

But Kathy can be brought back in a way that many people fail to realize. Of all life on earth, the human race is the only segment that possess memory. All we have to do is use our memory to bring Kathy, or anyone we have known, back-to create a living memory of her. We also have imagination and can use it to fix Kathy in any place, but not in any time. She remains as we remember her.

The best feature of a memory regeneration is that your subjects never change even though you grow old. You can always see Kathy as you knew her and recall any incident that your memory permits.

In my history related to the Parks family are related many incidents involving the form that memory takes. One recurrent memory, involved a young girl of twenty (Kathy's age), when I was twenty-one. At the age of seventy-seven, I found myself traveling near where she was living and decided to call on her. Remember I had not seen her since 1911-57 years previously. As I was searching for her house, the thought suddenly struck me, "What am I looking for? What do I expect to find? S____ is 76 years of age and I'm looking for a girl of twenty!" I did not want to destroy that memory so turned around.

That's the way I want to remember Kathy. That's the way you and I who knew her will remember her. She will never grow old to you and she will never see you as you fade away. It's not life as you are now living it, but still it's part of life because you make use of one of your natural attributes to bring her back-your memory. Why not visit with her occasionally. Who knows? She may welcome your visit.

"She has put on invisibility.
Dear Lord, I cannot see-
But this I know, although the road ascends
And passes from my sight
That there will be no night;
That you will take her gently by the hand
And lead her on
Along the road of life that never ends,
And she will find it is not death but dawn.
I do not doubt that You are there as here,
And You will hold her dear...."
From "The Traveler" by James Dillet Freeman

WILDWOOD INN
INVESTIGATION REPORT

What follows are various Colorado reports that will be of interest to all readers of the Bundy case, for they give an interesting look into various aspects of the investigation, and being case file material, it contains information that rarely gets into the books.

When I was writing about the abduction of Caryn Campbell from the Wildwood Inn for my book, *The Bundy Murders: A Comprehensive History*, I worked closely with retired Colorado investigator, Michael J. Fisher, who gave me the inside story what it was like to piece together what had happened to Caryn on that cold early evening of January 12, 1975. Indeed, this story was so interesting to readers, that when I was writing *The Trail of Ted Bundy: Digging Up the Untold Stories*, published in 2016, I included almost all of Mike's communications to me so the reader can see them in his own words. And beyond this, there's not a lot more that can be said of *his* investigation at the Wildwood Inn.

However, the technical information of the actual search of the inn conducted by officers is very interesting indeed. What follows is from the official record detailing the extensive search of the Wildwood Inn, and while it may seem a bit repetitive as to the actions taken, it will give the reader the unglamourous and repetitive (but exceedingly important) side of law enforcement when conducting such investigations.

Author's note: because there are numerous names that are not capitalized, and a lack of capitalization at the beginning of various sentences (as well as other grammatical errors), I have corrected all of these for purposes of clarity. And because it's the official record, other, non-grammatical mistakes, are left as they appear, but in some cases I will make note of it and provide an explanation as needed.

1/12/75 Complaint-offense report Pitkin County Sheriff's Department

Time 10:30 p.m. Sunday officers Carson/Weiditz Report taken at 10:47 p.m. Disappearance at approximately 8:00 p.m.

Both officers were dispatched to room 210 of the Wildwood Inn on a missing-person report. Upon arrival we did contact the complainant who relayed the following to us. The woman who was traveling with him, Ms. Campbell, 23 years of age, 5ft 4in tall, 105 pounds brown shoulder-length hair, last seen wearing a beige woolly jacket and blue jeans, had left the doctor and his two children in the lobby of the Wildwood Inn and went back to their room, room 210, to retrieve a magazine. The young lady had not returned as of this point. It should be indicated that doctor G and Miss Campbell had been living together for one year. Miss Campbell is a registered nurse, has no history of any mental problems, is not on any medication or drugs. Dr. G and Miss Campbell and his children had been in Aspen for about two days. They had planned on leaving January 19, 1975. And attempted to locate (*Author's note: this should read "An attempt to locate…"*) was aired by this officer at approximately 11:25 p.m.

1/13/75 Supplementary Report-Detective sergeant William Baldridge and Foss-Suspected homicide.

Page 1

Reporting officer between 10:30 a.m. and 2:30 this date did with Detective Sergeant Baldridge conduct an investigation into the disappearance of one Karen E. Campbell from the Wildwood Inn. The disappearance did take place at approximately 10:00 p.m. (*Author's note: this is incorrect. Her abduction occurred between 7:30 and 8:00 p.m.*) on January 12, 1975.

Reporting officers did conduct with a Mr. Robert D Gile Jr. who is president of the Wildwood Inn, a thorough physical search of the Wildwood Inn, reporting officer began the search in the basement and boiler area with negative results. Reporting officer and Mr. Gile did then search the ground floor area as follows:

1. The Max Convention room and all storage rooms adjacent to it.

2. Both the male and female restrooms.

3. The telephone switching room.

4. The trash bin on the exterior of the building directly adjacent to the main luggage room.

5. The elevator shaft.

All of the above areas yielded negative results. Reporting officer and Mr. Kyle (*Author's note: with no formal introduction of a Mr. Kyle, this may again be a reference to Mr. Gile.*) then searched the first floor as follows:

1. The upper Powderhorn card room

2. All key storage areas

3. The first-floor vending machine room

4. Room 167, directly adjacent to the elevator which was vacant and had been vacant since December 28, 1974

While in the room reporting officer did observe both beds had been slept in. There were several cups with coffee residue on the dresser. An ashtray containing several cigarette butts was on the nightstand between the beds. It is the reporting officer's observation this room had been occupied for at least 24 hours prior to this date. *(Author's note: over the years I have heard from a number of people who've suggested that Bundy either may have had a room at the Wildwood, may have had Caryn in it, or may have returned to the room after dumping Caryn Campbell on the snowy frigid ground 2.8 miles away from the inn. And while I'm not certain if this is the information my sources are referring to, let's for a moment consider it. First, if Bundy was in this room, it is unknown how he could have made entry, and frankly, it might have been next to impossible. Far easier to believe (in my opinion) is that it was an employee of the hotel doing a friend a favor. In truth, it could have been a number of scenarios. Even so, it's interesting to speculate, and since it cannot hurt, let's see what Bundy would have done, or not done, if he had this room for a time, and ultimately what we know positively because of what Bundy himself said about it.*

First, there isn't any way Bundy would have had Caryn Campbell in that room, it just logistically couldn't have happened. What Bundy told Mike Fisher on his second interview on Sunday night, January 20, 1989 (his first session with Bundy was on Saturday the 19th, where he and Colorado detective, Matt Lindvall sat down with the killer) is that Caryn wasn't Bundy's first choice that evening. What follows is from my book, The Bundy Murders: A Comprehensive History, second edition:

"However, as Caryn walked across the balcony, she spotted through the wafting steam from the outdoor heated pool (the steam, which acted like a moving cloud, would reveal people and then quickly shroud them again), a man using crutches while holding ski boots, who appeared to be in need of assistance. Being a kind woman as well as a nurse, Caryn called down to Bundy and asked if he

needed help. Bundy, who'd been trying to get the attention of a woman near the pool who he hoped would help him to his car, quickly said yes. And as he would later tell an investigator just before his execution, as they reached the car (and no doubt as Caryn was placing the crutches into the VW), he hit her with the ski boots and knocked her out cold. Not one person saw the two leave the inner portion of the Wildwood Inn, or take the short walk down the steps where they'd continue the short distance to the parking lot situated on the side of the building. Once inside the VW, or shortly thereafter, he would hit Caryn once in the head with the crowbar, and this produced an extensive amount of cranial damage that, without question, rendered her unconscious for most, if not all the time Bundy had possession of her."

Knowing this, it's clear Bundy couldn't have taken her to this room, and he was very forthright as to what he did to Caryn and where. That said, would he have returned to this room as some consider? Absolutely, if that's what he wanted to do. Indeed, through the writing of my books on Bundy, I have mentioned more than once how Bundy's desires could change at any moment, and when this occurred, even during a murder, he would, if he so desired, depart from his usual Modus Operandi on nothing more than a personal and momentary whim. So too, we must remember he felt impervious to detection and apparently never had any real or on-going fear of being apprehended. However, the question remains: did Bundy, even if he had somehow secured this room, would he have returned to the Wildwood Inn that night; all the while Dr. Gadowski was searching with his two children for Caryn, or when the police were called and soon thereafter arrived on the scene? It's certainly possible, but in my opinion, unlikely. The only way he would have returned is if he wanted to (we're speaking here of Bundy's strange mindset pertaining *to his murders and the invincibility of detection he believed he possessed), 'rub it in their faces' so to speak. At that point, anything is possible with Bundy, and nothing is off the proverbial table.*

Lastly, while we're on the murder of Caryn Campbell, and Mike Fisher's last conversation with Bundy on Sunday January 20, 1989, here's a portion of his communication to me that was published in The Trail of Ted Bundy: Digging Up the Untold Stories:

Of the actual murder of Caryn Campbell, Bundy told Mike the following:

"Took her like I took the other one (Julie) I took her from the hotel after she got out of the elevator..." "I took her to where you found her, and everything happened there..." He was referring to the Owl Creek Road. Questioning Theodore asking him for details was not getting me the icing I wanted on my cake...he was general. I asked him how he killed her, and he responded "Just like the others..."

I had to ask him again how many times had he struck her, and he replied "Just once, I did my thing right there in the car..." While picking for details of area, he told me "....it was a snowy road; very slick I took her over the bank to where I guess you found her..." I asked if he knew if she was alive when he "put her where I found her," he looked at me like I had asked him to pass the sugar and said, "I don't know." Total indifference, he was through with her.

(Author's note: People well versed in the Bundy the case will know that on Saturday, January 21, 1989, Mike Fisher, along with Colorado detective, Matt Lindvall, sat down with Bundy and recorded his final confession concerning the murders he committed in Colorado. However, most are not aware that on Sunday night, January 22, 1989, Fisher again sat down with Bundy and conducted an interview that lasted between twenty or thirty minutes. The interview was not recorded and they mostly discussed the abduction and murder of Caryn Campbell.)

We will now continue with the report...

5. The pool area which is located between the east west south wing of the Wildwood Inn

6. Both male and female sunrooms located to the west of the swimming pool

7. All areas adjacent to the exterior of the Wildwood Inn on the first-floor level

8. The laundry room and adjacent crawl spaces. All areas checked negative

Reporting officer (*Author's note: 'returned' was the word likely left out by mistake in this report*) and then proceeded to the second floor and searched the following:

1. The Wildwood sales office

2. Liquor storage area

3. Room 266 which was vacant and everything appeared to be in order

4. Rooms 254 and 252 both were vacant and appeared to be in order

5. The second-floor vending machine

6. The second-floor maid's closet

7. All walkways and trash cans on or around the exterior of the second floor.

All areas checked negative.

RO and Mr. Geila (*Author's note: yes, the spelling has changed once again*) then proceeded to the third floor and searched the following:

1. Room 308 which was vacant and in order

2. Room 366 vacant and in order

3. Trash bin behind the wineskin restaurant

4. The third-floor vending machine room

5. The third-floor maid's closet

All rooms checked negative

Baldridge and Mr. Guile then proceeded to the fourth and final level where we searched the following:

1. Room 407, which was vacant. Everything appeared to be in order.

2. Room 404 which was vacant and in order

3. Room for 414 and 413 vacant and in order

4. 4th floor vending machine room

5. 4th floor maid's closet

All areas checked negative

Reporting officer did also check all exterior grounds and accessible roofs with negative results. Reporting officer did talk with the waitress at the Stew Pot who has served the complaint and Miz see shortly (*Author's note: a total foul up of the language here*) before Miss Campbell's disappearance. The waitress stated that she had observed no arguments or heated discussion taking place between either party during the time they were in the restaurant. Reporting officer then checked the Aspen Ski School located to the east of the Snowmass mall to see if Miss Campbell had taken or was signed up to take lessons. Negative end of report cases status open.

TYING UP LOOSE ENDS

What you're about to read should have gone in my sixth Bundy book, *The Enigma of Ted Bundy*. The reason it didn't is because, amidst all the other things I was compiling for the book, it slipped my mind. Even so, this is a good place to set the record straight.

I will be addressing the myth that Ted Bundy grew up believing that Louise was his sister and his grandparents were his parents. True, there apparently was some confusion in the child's mind for a brief time. However, this occurred when Bundy was either three or four-years-old. And it is most assuredly true that by the time he and his mother Louise forever left Philadelphia for Washington State when Teddy was around five years old, he understood that Louise was his mother.

It's more than a bit baffling to me that this myth that Ted grew up still believing Louise was his sister, some believing into his teenage years, which is absurd. Indeed, the facts pertaining to what the boy's life was like, and how he perceived his family and surroundings, is clear from the known facts; and the facts are as follows:

When Louise met Johnnie Bundy and the two decided to get married, Johnnie was well aware that Ted was her son. As such, instead of raising him as a stepson, Johnnie adopted him and gave him the name Bundy. Over the years, Johnnie and Louise had four children, and all the kids grew up knowing that Ted was their brother. Ted also had two best friends as a young boy, Terry Storwick and Warren Dodge, and they understood Ted was the son of Louise. No one ever believed that Ted Bundy was anything other than the son of Louise Bundy and the adopted son of Johnnie. And again, all of this information has been available for decades, yet in some circles the myth continues.

On a final note, I asked Mike McCann if, in his years of dealing with Bill Hagmaier, did he ever ask him if Bundy talked about this myth, and Mike said that Hagmaier told him Bundy referred to it as "BS".

LET'S TALK EVIDENCE
ONE MORE TIME

For those of you who've read my last book, *The Enigma of Ted Bundy*, you're aware I've discussed topics that some find controversial; topics such as: did Ted Bundy keep living victims in his second-floor apartment at 565 First Avenue in Salt Lake City, Utah? Did Bundy sever the heads of some of his victims? These subjects I covered in my book, *The Bundy Murders: A Comprehensive History*, because it's clear from the record that both of these things are true. That said, some folks have a tendency to not believe it.

Indeed, it reminds me of how convinced so many were that Ted's grandfather, Samuel Cowell, was also his father. I remember asking one woman why she believed this, and she responded, "I just know it's true!". Well, despite the very strong feeling of those who believe this, it was all finally put to rest when DNA analysis proved that Sam Cowell was not the father of Ted Bundy. It would be far better for folks to say, "Well, it may be true", but until we have some evidence to show Cowell was his father, it's unwise to be dogmatic about such things. To be sure, incest is real, and if the analysis would show Sam Cowell to be the father, that might have explained a great deal (in the minds of many), why Bundy became a vicious killer of women and young girls.

Anyway, Bill Hagmaier, of the BSU (Behavioral Science Unit) spent some 200 hours interviewing Bundy between 1986 and Bundy's execution in 1989. Bundy confided many things to Bill, and many of these revelations have been put into FBI government reports. What follows is from the Bundy Multi-Agency Investigative Report. A note: I will be duplicating only a small portion of the report that covers Bundy's severing of heads and whether or not he took victims to his Utah apartment; as well as some other interesting info pertaining to certain aspects of the murders and his disposal of the bodies. For those wanting a closer look at the Multi-Agency Report, it is readily available on the Internet.

Of the thirty victims BUNDY claimed to have killed, he reportedly buried about ten. He would always attempt to bury the bodies two or three feet deep and place rocks on top of the grave. He also claimed to have disposed of victims in bodies of water.

BUNDY reported he severed the heads of about a dozen of his victims. He would sometimes retain the heads for longer periods than the bodies and not necessarily dispose of the body and head in the same location. Actually, body parts, clothing, and other victim possessions were dispersed, perhaps, hundreds of miles from the discarded torso.

BUNDY clearly followed media reports of his crimes as well as the reports of others who killed. He was interested in other people's murders and the possibility he was being copied. He followed his own cases to glean as much intelligence as possible regarding suspects, evidence, leads, etc. He felt he was helped quite a bit with the abundance of information from the investigators' quotes available through the media and his perceived lack of cooperation among law enforcement agencies.

Although ligature strangulation was BUNDY's favorite method of killing, the manual strangulation of his first murder is consistent behavior in an evolving serial murderer. That is, a serial killer is disorganized when he starts but improves significantly as he progresses, choosing his victims, murder and strangle her with a ligature while raping her. Although his first murder was reportedly performed by beating and manual strangulation, he most often used a ligature he had prepared solely for that purpose. Victims were strangled from the rear.

Being voyeuristic, it was important that BUNDY be able to see what he was doing. He selected sites where the moon shone brightly, or he would "operate" in front of the headlights of his vehicle. He commented that there were times he thought he should have been caught because the headlights of his vehicle would have been visible to people driving in the area.

There is little evidence to indicate BUNDY recorded his murders or assaults in any particular fashion. He indicated he had, at one time, a box of polaroid photographs of victims that he kept hidden but subsequently destroyed after becoming a suspect. It is known he would sometimes keep ski brochures that were apparently marked to signify homicides. Also found was a brochure from the high school play where one of his victims was abducted. BUNDY advised he would discard everything belonging to his victims and would sometimes discard his possessions, such as his props or tools, connected with the incidents. He would later have to replace those items.

BUNDY gave the impression that he committed most of the assaults outdoors, except in Utah and Florida. In Utah, he was able to take his victims back to his apartment...

...At times BUNDY would feel the urge to kill when he had not done this planning and was not in his "predator mode". His victims, then, were often hitchhikers. In those cases, BUNDY was unable to be of much help to law enforcement since he did not know the victims' names and was often not able to pinpoint body disposal sites.

A note on the assertion that Bundy kept living victims in his Utah apartment: when I was writing *The Bundy Murders*, I said that while we can't "prove it", Bundy kept some of his victims inside his 565 First Avenue apartment. I based this on first, Mike Fisher's (the Colorado investigator) belief that Bundy kept them on the grounds, and perhaps in the utility room (Bundy was acting apartment manager, renting rooms as well as cutting the grass, etc.). The second reason has to do with Bundy's own words to the writer, Stephen Michaud, which convinced me beyond doubt that he indeed kept some, or at least one, of his victims inside his room, and more about that in a minute.

But back to the utility room. It didn't make sense to me that Bundy would keep them in the utility room, as there wasn't enough room to do those things he wanted to do, and as such, pulling what I now call a "Lynda Ann Healy move in reverse", Bundy must have taken them up to his 2nd floor apartment, likely in the middle of the night, and this would go along with what Michaud said. Here he would be free to do whatever he wanted to do in much better comfort, and especially so as Bundy may have had both Melissa Smith and Laura Ann Aime each for a number of days as I explained in the book. At the time of this writing (2006-2008), I wasn't aware a cellar existed on the property, so I wasn't thinking about a possible third location where Bundy may have housed them. Interestingly, I do remember seeing the covering to this cellar in the rear of the home in 2006 and again in 2015, and it's on the opposite side of where Bundy's apartment was located (if you're standing in the rear of the house, the entrance to the cellar is on the right), and I never considered this location might enter in to what Bundy did with the (as we now know) four victims he brought to his apartment.

Of course, once I heard about the cellar, and was made aware that a resident of the rooming house would sometimes hear Bundy moving around down there late at night, we can say with absolute certainty that Bundy did keep *some* of his victims there, and in my mind, two of the victims likely taken there were Debra Kent, whom Bundy kept only until the day after her abduction (Bundy later admitted on tape that he killed her there), and Nancy Wilcox, whom he also brought to his apartment for around 24 hours.

So, the question is this: would he keep more long-term abductees in that cellar? Well, it's certainly possible, and in my mind, would it not be for what he shared with Michaud, I would think yes, perhaps the cellar is key to all of this. However, when one looks at what Bundy said (in the third-person he understood he could speak freely), I must say, that in my mind, he must have taken some or at least one of his victims to his room, due to the egregious risks he admitted to taking. Indeed, pulling his VW up to his apartment and parking in the rear of the building, perhaps directly in front of where the cellar is located, would not be as risky as some might think; especially in the dead of night and if Bundy saw no lights on and the area was free of activity. At such a moment, Bundy would simply get out, unlock the cover to the cellar and lift the lid. Then, looking around to see that the proverbial coast is clear, simply raise the trunk lid, located in the front of the VW, and within a matter of seconds, have his victim down the steps. This, in my opinion, does not constitute that same type of risk he was revealing to Stephen Michaud, and as such, I believe his apartment became part of his "lair" as well. Of course, if I ever discover where Bundy actually admitted to someone (Bill Hagmaier, perhaps?) that he never had any victims in his upstairs Utah apartment, then we'll have a definitive answer to this much-debated question. And if that ever happens, why then did he make such a statement to Stephen Michaud?

What follows is only a portion about this from *The Enigma of Ted Bundy*, but it illustrates perfectly what I'm talking about. SM is Stephen Michaud, TB is Bundy:

SM: There's perhaps a lack of sophistication on my part. Having to go in and out of residences with any large bundle would seem to be risking everything, no matter what time of day...

TB: This person taking bundles in, in and out of his house or his apartment. We say in retrospect, that was really chancy. But there were times when I think he... he almost felt as if he were immune from detection. Not in a mystical or a spiritual sense or anything, but that on occasion he felt like he could walk through doors. He didn't feel like he was, uh, invisible or anything like that. But at times he felt that no matter how much he fucked up, nothing could go wrong. The boldness was probably a result of not being rational. Of just being moved by a situation—not really thinking it out clearly, and not even seeing risks. But just overcome by that boldness and desire to accomplish a particular thing. Only in retrospect would he wonder how he managed to succeed in spite of some of those rash and bold acts.

AFTERWORD

This concludes the first volume of the new series, *Ted Bundy: The Yearly Journal*. The next installment will occur in about a year. For those who follow me on Facebook, or my author page at WildBlue Press, in the coming months, I'll be posting tidbits about the new information that's coming to light, as well as certain other aspects of the case worth covering in far greater detail in volume two.

One tidbit I can give you now so you'll have something to think about in the coming months, has to do with Evergreen State College, where Bundy abducted Donna Manson as she walked from her dorm to the library for a jazz concert. During the research phrase for *The Bundy Murders*, I was made aware of another attempted abduction by Bundy, but I chose not to add it to the book as I was writing only about the known murders at the time. However, I will be investigating this attempted abduction and others he's likely responsible for.

In the end, we must remember that there is great deal we know about Bundy and the terrible things he did. On the flip side, however, there are a number of mysteries out there, just waiting to be discovered. As I look back on all the previous Bundy books I've written, and think about the astounding stories that have surfaced and discoveries made over the years, giving us factual information on Bundy that we didn't have before, makes all of my efforts focused on Bundy for so many years, completely and totally worthwhile. And thankfully, there's still that proverbial wind to my back, aiding me in my quest to know more, and as such, I look forward with great expectation to all the discoveries that lie ahead.

PHOTOS

Kathy Parks

The incarcerated Bundy on his way to court, 1976

Ted Bundy's tools of the trade of murder

The Wildwood Inn, where Bundy snatched
Caryn Campbell on January 12, 1975

Ted Bundy's rooming house in Salt Lake City

The steps leading up to Bundy's second floor apartment

In 1974, this was Bundy's apartment, marked number 2

The steps leading down from the pool at the Wildwood Inn. Bundy and Caryn Campbell may have taken these steps and then turned left, making the short walk to the parking lot where he assaulted her while she was placing crutches into his VW.

Because Bundy was a planner of murder, he may have lead Caryn Campbell out this side entrance, which would have taken them through an enclosed passageway and directly into the parking lot. And if this area was void of foot traffic that early evening, this would be the easiest way for Bundy to abduct her.

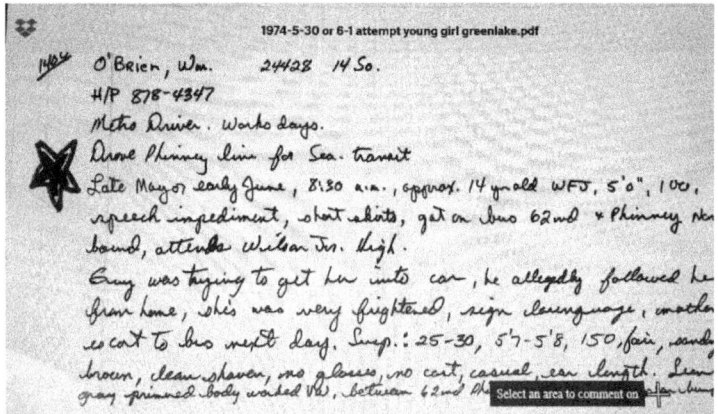

King County Police report describing a man following a 14-year-old girl and attempting to get her into his car. Geographically, this is very close to where Bundy attempted to abduct Michele Komen, also 14, who refused to enter his car. Courtesy, Mike McCann

Bundy, looking introspective, and in the hands of the Utah authorities, circa 1976

Chapter One

The Official Record

Author's note: Because this is the official record, I have left it as it is, without corrections in grammar or those things an editor would do when going over a manuscript.

It is important to publish the record as it appears. However, I will note where mistakes are located, as well as occasionally correct a misspelling, as I did with the misspelling of Liz Kloepfer's name. Outside of these noted corrections, the record remains the same as you can see them in the archives today.

Ballantyne Supplementary Report
Attempt to Locate Monday Jan. 26, 1976

On Sunday, January 25, 1976, this officer received a call from Chief Dean O. Anderson stating that Mr. Richard Maughan had called him and advised that Margaret Maughan, his daughter, had some information about the Bundy case.

At 2:30 P.M. on 1/25/76 this officer and Chief Anderson met with Richard and Margaret Maughan in Chief Anderson's office. The following is the substance of Margaret's information.

Margaret stated that she had talked with Ted Bundy and they conversed about the tear in the back seat of Ted's Volkswagen. Ted Stated they can't get me on that because a lot of Volkswagen's have torn back seats. Margaret stated to this officer that she noticed the tear in the back seat just before Ted sold the car and the stuffing was coming out of it.

Ted also advised that he didn't believe there was a difference between right and wrong, and that he liked virgins and he could get sex with them anytime he wanted to.

Margaret advised that the front seat in Ted's Volkswagen was loose and when you rode in it you had to hang on because the seat would rock.

I asked Margaret when she had last seen Ted and she stated just before Christmas. She advised at that time he was supporting a full beard. I asked her if Ted wore glasses often and she stated no but when he does, he wears different types. When asked if Ted had to wear glasses, she stated she didn't know.

Margaret advised that she has talked with a newspaper reporter from Seattle by the name of Henderson (first name unknown) but he writes for the night paper. Mr. Henderson advised that he and Ted had taken a trip down the river in Seattle in a boat. Tied behind the boat was a innertube which a girl was riding on. The boat hit some rough water and according to Henderson, Bundy got a wild look in his eyes and untied the innertube. Henderson further stated that Bundy drove like a wild man back to Seattle, and never said a word for the entire hour and one half.

Further Henderson told Margaret that someone had written down the Washington plate number that is on Ted's truck in an abduction in Oregon.

I asked Margaret if she knew whether Ted had ever been to Colorado and she stated that he had been over to one of the ski resorts.

Ted further told Margaret that he had asked a Carl Weary (spelling unknown) to watch his apartment for him when he left town because he was fearful that the police might try to break in. Ted obtained a heavy lock for the door, put screws in the windows and pulled the ladder up from the window. Margaret will obtain the date this happened.

Ted further advised that he had taken a trip over Lambs Canyon and had come out in Provo in the fall in 1974 prior to the snowfall. I asked Margaret if she knew of it was before or after the disappearance of Debra Kent, but she didn't know.

(Author's note: what follows is a Bountiful Police report, somewhat redacted, pertaining to a student taking a phone call at Viewmont High School in the days following the abduction of Debra Kent (by Ted Bundy) which occurred

on the evening of November 8, 1974. It is an odd call, and in this writer's opinion, it's just the thing Ted Bundy would do. After this incident, the rest of the report continues)

BOUNTIFUL POLICE DEPARTMENT
Supplementary Report
Wednesday, Nov. 13, 1974.
I interviewed Pam at Viewmont High School and she stated that she works in the office and that at approximately 11:45 A.M. she stated that she received a telephone call from an individual that sounded like an older person, who wanted to know whether or not Debra KENT was at school or if she was on the absentee list. She was asked three of four times by this individual if Debra was at school.

Supplementary Report
Friday, September 5, 1975
Case No. 9340-74
COMPLAINANT: DEAN KENT
Reporting officer, Sgt. Collard, LT. Ballantyne wen to Salt Lake in an effort to locate the car belonging to Theodore Bundy in an effort to have the car observed by Carol DaRonch (*Author's note: Carol DaRonch, whom Bundy abducted from the Fashion Place Mall, and who shortly afterward escaped from her attacker.*)

The car was located at suspects residence. At this time Sgt. Collard went to pick up Carol. Prior to his arrival the vehicle left his residence, went to the university, back to his residence and then down to the telephone office on 200 South and 300 East.

Just shortly prior to Sgt. Collard's return to the area the vehicle left westbound on 200 South. Reporting officer followed and the vehicle turned north on Main Street.

Reporting officer was caught in a red light and hemmed in by traffic.

Prior to reporting officer's arrival on Main Street, the vehicle disappeared and this officer was unable to locate the vehicle. This officer checked all known possible locations again and was unable to locate the vehicle.

Reporting officer will attempt to relocate this vehicle again and attempt to have the witness look at the vehicle.

Supplementary Report
Wednesday, September 17, 1975
Case # 9340-74
COMPLAINANT: DEAN KENT
VICTIM: DEBRA KENT

This is an interview of Elizabeth Kloepfer (redacted). She works at the University of Washington Medical Institute. Elizabeth goes by the name of Liz.

Elizabeth was asked when she first became concerned about Ted and as to why she became concerned about him and thought that he might possibly been involved with some of the girls that had been slain in the Seattle area. She stated that she first became concerned because he resembled the composite which had been produced in the Seattle area and in following the newspaper reports she discovered the days the girls turned up missing he was not with her on any of these days.

She stated in October a girl friend of hers whose name is unknown at this time had visited Utah. Upon returning from Utah told her about a similar incident in the Salt Lake area which involved a missing girl very closely resembling that of the ones in the Seattle area. At this time Liz contacted the Seattle Police and advised them of Ted Bundy and asked them to contact the Salt Lake Police and talk with them in regards to him.

She stated that later another girl turned up missing in the Salt Lake area, this one as she recalled approximately Christmas time. At that time, she contacted her dad who was in Ogden, requested he call Salt Lake County Sheriff's Office and inform them of her suspicions. He had told her at this time that he did not wish to do this as he had no evidence and did not wish to become involved with the situation. She stated that when he informed her, he would not do this she herself called Captain Hayward and spoke with him at that time.

Liz was then asked if she knew where Ted received his money for his schooling and other bills. She stated that she did not know for sure. As far as she knew just from jobs he had.

This officer inquired as to whether or not his parents supplied some of the money. She stated she did not think so as they were not wealthy people and his father works as a cook at the Madison (*Author's note: Madigan*) Army Hospital and his mother works as a secretary at the hospital (*Author's note: University*) at Puget Sound and they live on a moderate income.

Liz was asked if she thought Ted was being truthful with her. She stated no. She was asked as to why she thought this. She stated that she knew he had lied to her in the past. She stated he has stolen items in the past such as a television and a stereo, a bicycle and possibly other items and at that time he had lied to her.

She was asked if she knew when he had purchased the vehicle, the Volkswagen, he is presently driving. She stated he had owned the car since approximately 1972. She stated the color was a light beige at the time.

She stated he purchased a white Ford pickup truck which he has presently in the Salt Lake area about one year ago before he left for Salt Lake City. (*Author's note: I was recently told that the white truck went with Bundy to his 364 Douglas Avenue residence, and that the vehicle remained in the rear of the home, and perhaps in the garage, for quite some time after Bundy was incarcerated.)* She was asked if she had ever gone skiing with Ted. She said she had gone skiing one time at Snow Basin; however, she could not remember the date. She also drove up to Snow Bird with him last year, however, it was too crowded and they did not go skiing. She was asked when the last time was that she saw him and she stated in August of 1975. She was asked if at that time they had gone to the Park City area. She stated they had not. She did state, however, they had spent some time at Flaming Gorge at her dad's trailer.

She was asked if he liked the outdoors and she stated he did like the outdoors very much. Liz was asked if Ted had asked her anything about any of the girls that had been slain. She stated that he knew he was a suspect in the slaying of some of the girls in the Washington area and that he has known this for approximately 10 days to two weeks as someone has been in contact with him from the Washington area who has been contacted by the Seattle area police. She was then asked if he had said anything to her in regards to being a possible suspect in any of the girls in the Utah area. She stated he had not.

She was then asked if she knew whether Ted travelled much. She stated he was not much of a traveler. As far as she knew he did not travel very much at all. She was then asked if she was very close to him. She stated she was very close indicating that they had in the past had sexual relations. She was asked if over the past year he had changed and she stated no.

She was then asked if she felt he sometimes had two different personalities or acted like two different people. Her response was I think he is now. She was asked why. She stated that she has of late seen a side of him which is very cold and calculated. Liz was asked about how her father got along with him or what her father thought of him. Liz stated her father gets along well with him; however, he thinks he is just an opportunist that is taking her for a ride. When asked if she felt this way she stated well, he always ate at her house and at that time, they talked of plans for the future, which would include plans for marriage.

Liz was asked how long she had worn her hair in the style she is presently wearing it which is long, dark brown hair parted in the middle approximately shoulder blade length. She stated she has worn this for approximately the last six years as long as she has known Ted.

She was asked if he liked the way she wore her hair. She stated that she had at different times stated she was going to cut it which he became somewhat upset stating he liked it that way and not to cut it. She also stated that he had dated one other girl she knew and she also had long dark hair.

Liz was then asked if there were any unusual sex hang ups that she was aware of. Her first response was he has a normal sex life and then went on to elaborate that at the end of 1973 he asked her one night if he could tie her up for the sex act, that he used her nylon socks to tie her with and laying her on the bed he tied her legs spread apart and then tied her arms and hands. She stated that he also developed a liking for anal intercourse during this same period of time.

She stated that she only allowed him to tie her up a couple of times but the last time he tied her up while they were in the act of their sexual relations that he placed his hands around her throat choking and hurting her, however, at that time she did not say anything to him in regards to this, however, she refused to be tied up any more after that. She stated he had obtained these ideas from reading a book which he had purchased by the name of "Joy of Sex".

She stated that one thing that bothered her was that during the summer of 1974 that his sex drive dropped to near zero. She stated that one possible explanation was that he was working quite hard and was tired a lot of the time. She stated she had confronted him as to whether he was possibly having an affair with other girls to which he stated no.

Liz also stated that one day as she entered his apartment, she found a brown paper sack in the middle of the floor just inside his apartment door and she noticed one of the items in the sack was a woman's bra, however, she did not go through the sack any further. When asked why, she stated she did not know, maybe she was possibly embarrassed or scared to do this. She stated this was in the fall of 1973. She stated she did not ever say anything to him about it and he did not ever say anything to her.

Liz was asked if Ted had any knives. She stated he always had knives. When asked what kind of knives she stated he had an oriental type knife which was in a wood sheath which he kept in the glove compartment of her car for several months. At one time she had asked him what it was and he stated it was just a knife that a friend had given him.

She also stated he had a meat cleaver in his apartment that he kept with his other cooking utensils. Liz was then asked if there were any other unusual items, she knew of in his apartment that she did not know he had. She stated she had found some plaster of Paris which would be used for a cast possibly. When she stated when she asked him why and where it came from he stated it was something he swiped from a medical supply house he worked for near the University of Washington. She also stated he had a pair of crutches. When she confronted him with them, he stated they were the landlord's and he had left them in his apartment.

Liz stated she had received a phone call from Ted last date in the evening. She was then asked if he had mentioned anything about Salt Lake or the police in Salt Lake. She stated he had. She had confronted him in regards to his arrest and he became quite upset because of her knowing it. He stated the police had contacted Seattle and Seattle was doing some checking on him and the police in Salt Lake were harassing him. He stated the officer that arrested him was out to get him and was just plain harassing him.

She stated he also said that the police had over-stepped their bounds and he was not worried about the charge he was picked up on because it was an illegal search (*Author's note: notice he's not saying he's not worried because he's innocent, only that they made a mistake - which they didn't - and it's a technical issue.*)

Liz then inquired as to whether all the items were together in a bag indicating the handcuffs, the ski mask, etc. She was told in the affirmative. She stated that she had confronted him in regards to the items she knew were in the bag and that he had told her he used the ski mask to keep his ears warm while he was shoveling snow as it was cold. She did not know at that time about the handcuffs or some of the other items in the bag.

Liz was then asked if she knew whether Ted wore patent leather shoes very often. She stated she never knew him to wear patent leather shoes at all. She was then asked if she had ever known Ted to wear a mustache. She stated she has known him to wear a full beard, however, never a mustache alone. She did state however he always had a fake mustache. When asked what style she described a brush type. She stated he had owned this ever since she has known him for approximately the last six years, and that he usually carries it with him. When asked why he had it she stated he sometimes wears it to act cool.

Liz was then asked if she knew of the rip in the backseat of Ted's car and she stated it had been there approximately one year. She was asked if she knew it was fixed and stated she did not. She stated he was planning on selling his vehicle to help pay for his tuition and lawyer. She stated when he talked with her last date he also asked her to send him $700.00 to help pay for his lawyer. She then stated she inquired of him why he was carrying a crowbar in his car. He stated he always carries a crowbar and in fact he stated he used it the day before he was stopped and did not state what for. She stated she asked him why he had run from the officer. She indicated he told her that he had been drinking beer and didn't want to stop.

Liz was then asked where Ted had resided prior to his coming to the Seattle area. She stated he had been in Philadelphia for a while approximately seven or eight years ago going to a university there.

Liz was then shown a picture of a girlfriend in the Salt Lake area of Ted's and asked if she knew her. She stated no. She then asked is she a close friend of his. She was informed that it is thought that she is.

She stated then that Ted in his conversation with her had indicated that the police in Salt Lake knew he was coming to Seattle to sell his car and he was wondering how they knew. Liz was then asked if she knew Ted had joined the Mormon Church and she stated she did. He had told her the Missionaries had been on his back ever since he had got there and he had decided it was the right time to join.

Liz was then asked if she knew how he knew the police knew he was planning on coming to Seattle to sell his car. She stated she did not and the only possibility she could think of was possibly her old bishop as he had asked her how to contact him as he wanted him there for the baptism.

Liz stated he has called her several times this past week always telling her how much he really misses her, that he needs her and wants her to marry him. She stated he has not done this in the past and this seems unusual to her.

Liz was then asked if she would classify him as a schizophrenic and she stated I do now. She was then asked if she would classify him as being somewhat schizophrenic during the sex act and she said no. She was asked if she could think of anything else unusual. She stated in trying to think back and remember as near as she could recall she had received a phone call that she thought was a Friday night as near as she could remember which was the same night that one of the girls in the Salt Lake area disappeared, possibly, that of Debra Kent. She stated it was unusual for him to call from a pay phone.

She was asked if he had ever been violent and had ever hit her. She stated he had not. The only time he had hit her they had been out drinking one night, got into an argument and she stated go ahead and hit me and he did.

Liz was then asked if she knew if he owned a gun. She stated as far as she knew he did not. She was then asked if she knew of any unusual mental hang-ups that Ted might have and she stated the only thing she could think of was that he was an illegitimate child and that his mother had never told him. He had learned of it and he was quite embittered about this, however, she stated as far as she knew his mother did not know that he knew about this.

Liz was asked if she knew of any other things that Ted might of stolen. She stated one time a police officer came to her house stating that someone had pawned a stolen camera using her address. She stated it was described as a guy who at that time was with a blond girl and she is now wondering if Ted might have possibly been the one to pawned it.

Liz was then asked if she had any doubts in her mind in regards to Ted's activities. She stated she has a lot of doubts and she is definitely not sure and she at this time could in no way marry Ted and at this time any thoughts of marriage are out.

(*Author's note: what follows is a re-interview of Liz conducted the next day, September 18, 1975.*)

This is a re-interview of Elizabeth Kloepfer – known as Liz.

This took place at the University of Washington Hospital at 11:00 Hours 9/18/75

Interviewers were: Reporting officer and Detective Deputy Jerry Thompson.

Liz was asked as to her knowledge of the attitude toward police officers in general and she said Ted has a very good attitude and is usually praising police departments. Liz was then asked Ted's habits towards mixing with groups and she stated he mixes quite well, however, he does not have a lot of close male friends.

She was asked what type of sports he participated in and she stated tennis and handball. She stated she did not know of any other particular ones than this.

Liz was asked what contact she has had since September 1974 with Ted. She stated she has talked with him several times by telephone and in December 1974 at Christmas time she came to Salt Lake. In January of 1975 he visited in Seattle between quarters and in August of 1975 she again visited him in Salt Lake City. She stated while she was visiting him in December in Salt Lake, she learned Ted was smoking a lot of pot with his roommate or acquaintance that lived across the hall from him by the name of Scott. She stated this was always a problem between them after she learned it and they argued considerably about him using marijuana and the effects it could possibly have on him.

Liz then referred back to the picture which was shown in the last interview and asked if that girl's name was Gloria Ann or Glory Ann. She was told no it was not. She stated that he had developed a friendship with a girl by the name of Gloria A. who is a law student at the University of Utah as they worked together on several projects for class.

Liz was then asked if Ted had ever mentioned to her anything in regards to the missing girls, especially in the Washington area or Salt Lake area. She stated he has talked to her about the girls in the Washington area, however, he has not talked to her very much. He stated since the time he was arrested in Salt Lake he has talked to his ex-landlord in the Seattle area who had been contacted by the King County Sheriff's office in regards to a background check on Ted and that his landlord had told him he is being investigated in the possible disappearance of the girls. He stated he had discovered it is not a good thing to be named Ted in the Seattle area.

She stated he had contacted a friend of his by the name of Ann Rule who lives in Seattle and who writes crime stories for magazines and that Ann contacted King County to see what was going on and they told her it was strictly a routine investigation. She stated Ann re-contacted Ted and informed him of such.

She was asked if Ted had mentioned anything to her about the type of evidence the police had in regard to the disappearances and slayings of the girls and she stated he has not.

Liz was then asked if she had ever known Ted's car to be any other color than the beige color which it presently is. She stated she has not that it was beige when he got it. Liz was then asked if Ted ever mentioned any girls or types of girls which he does not like or any types particularly that he likes and she stated he has not.

Liz was then asked what her girlfriend's name was to which she had referred to previously that she had discussed this situation with. She gave the name as Mary Lynn Chino who lives at (redacted)...When Liz was asked if her girlfriend Mary Lynn had any doubts towards Ted, she stated Mary Lynn definitely has some doubts.

Liz was then asked again in reference to a raft which she stated Ted had. She stated he has a four-man yellow rubber raft which she had given to him as a graduation present when he graduated from the University of Washington.

Liz was then asked if Ted had ever mentioned being to Bountiful or knowing anyone in the Bountiful area and she stated he has not.

Liz was then questioned again in regards to the mustache. She stated it was a brown mustache. It was straight and quite sparse brush type and just came to the corner of the lips and did not drop at all.

In reference back to the night of 9/16/75 when Liz had talked with Ted, she stated he had lied to her about being arrested. But when she told him that she knew that he had been arrested he stated he had been arrested for speeding. She then informed him that she knew why he had been arrested and he became quite upset at her knowing. He then stated that after they had stopped him they had gone through his car looking for anything and everything to bust him on and he was surprised that they had not taken the fire extinguisher out of his car and charged him with arson also.

At the time Liz talked to him she did not know anything about the handcuffs and therefore did not ask him anything about it. Also, she stated that her car had been stolen for a few days in the summer of 1973 and was gone for two or three days and when the car was returned the oriental type knife in the wood sheath was missing at the time. She stated that Ted did drive her car occasionally.

Liz was then asked if Ted had ever been to California. She stated Ted had been to the San Francisco area in the spring of 1973 for a few days on business. She did not know anything more about his visit there.

Liz then stated one thing that struck her funny that she had talked with Ted in June (*Author's note; the transcriber typed J ne, so it must be assumed he meant to type June.*) and he was talking about hearing one report on the radio in regards to several rapes which had occurred in 1st Avenue in Salt Lake which is near the area he lives. The description of the guy involved was a guy with a beard and he stated to her I guess that lets me out. He stated that he thought a possible suspect was an individual that lives in a house for mentally retarded people around the corner from him which would be on F Street and that right after this description came out this individual shaved his beard and head. Liz, he stated, isn't that kind of funny (?). Liz stated that she told him not any funnier than a guy that is growing a beard. She stated Ted grew a beard in June 1975.

Liz then referred to a question that had been asked in an earlier interview in regards to two separate Ted's or schizophrenic personality. She stated that in thinking back Ted is very jealous of her. He follows her when she goes to various places or meetings to see who she is with or what she is doing. She stated he takes naps and sleeps a lot during the day and is out a lot late at night. She stated he used to sneak up on her when she was walking alone at night when she had no idea he was around and suddenly jump out of the bushes and grab her scaring the hell out of her.

She stated that this really made her angry. Liz referred back to the girls which were missing from the Seattle area stating that the only one she could really pin-point was one on July 14, 1974 which turned up missing shortly after she started becoming suspicious of Ted.

She stated on Saturday night they had been out and had argued. On Sunday morning she was starting to get ready for church and that Ted came over which surprised her due to the fact she thought he was mad at her. She stated he asked her where she was going to which she told him to church and then another place she was going and she thought he might meet her there, however, he did not. She stated approximately 6:00 PM that day he came over and asked her to go out to dinner with him. She stated at that time she had asked him where he had been as he looked very beat. He told her just laying around.

Liz was then asked as to her opinion of Ted's sexual activities, as to whether he as a very virile man was able to have repeated intercourse with only a few minutes in between. She stated when they first met he was able to perform very well, however, after six years of knowing him she stated she feels he is just a normal man. Liz was then shown a picture of the items which were confiscated from Ted's vehicle at the time of his arrest. She was asked if she had ever seen the crowbar before and she stated she had not and had no idea of his having it. She stated the only thing she has ever seen before is the gloves and the bag and the rest is foreign to her.

Liz stated that the items did look very suspicious and could cause some concern. Liz then stated there was another item which she could think of that might be somewhat suspicious. She stated when Ted used to drive her car around, she noticed he had taken her handle for the jack and had taped the one end of it. This being the end that curves slightly with adhesive tape and she had found this inside of her car a few times and not just in the truck area. She stated she had asked him as to why he had taped the handle and this occurred during the time there were student riots at the university and he stated with the riots you never know when you might need it.

She stated another incident that one night he was at her house, that he left, then came back shortly after. He returned to the porch and took something from an urn on the porch. She opened the door and observed the action but was unsure what it was and when she asked him what it was, he looked sick and tried to hide it from her. She stated she grabbed it from him discovering it was a pair of surgical gloves. She asked him what they were for and he just turned and left. This she said was one night late at night.

Liz then referred back to December and she had read or heard from somewhere that one of the individuals in the Salt Lake area was supposedly wearing a trench coat and when she flew into Salt Lake and Ted met her at the airport he was wearing his trench coat telling her how much he really liked it and enjoyed it. She stated she was quite struck when she saw him in the trench coat due to the fact that he had heard or read this previous to her coming down.

Liz then stated that after Ted learned that the police had talked with his landlord about him he called her and told her that if the police should try and contact her and talk to her that she was not to talk to them without first obtaining a lawyer. She stated she asked him what do I need a lawyer for, I haven't done anything wrong. She stated he told her that he just didn't want her to talk to the police without having an attorney present. (*Author's note: Bundy was thinking like a suspect here; suspects need attorneys when questioned by the police, not a couple of landlords merely answering questions about a former tenant. As if Ernst and Freda Rogers would put up a stumbling block between them and the police, and hire an attorney out of their own pocket. The truth of the matter is this: Ted Bundy spent his adult life asking things of people, be they favors or money, and whenever he felt like he could get away with it, would tell people what to do – for him! – and this is a perfect example.*)

Liz was then asked if Ted was a frequent visitor of the State Park where the girls disappeared in the Seattle area. She stated he was not. The only time she had ever known him to be there was approximately one week prior to the disappearance of the one girl (*Author's note: an obvious mistake here, the officer knowing -and stating above- that two women disappeared from the park*) from the state park area. She stated at that time he had gone there alone.

Liz then stated after having talked about the items which have been discussed in the interviews both yesterday and today her doubts are greatly increasing towards Ted and she wishes she could know for sure and at this time she has considerable doubts. She is of the opinion that there is a great possibility that Ted might be possibly involved in this.

Other Ted Bundy Books From Kevin Sullivan and WildBlue Press

"An important addition to true crime studies."
—Katherine Ramsland,
bestselling author of Psychopath.

the trail of
TED BUNDY

Digging
Up the
Untold
Stories

DIAGNOSTIC

KEVIN SULLIVAN
Author of The Bundy Murders

The Trail of Ted Bundy: A look into the life of serial killer Ted Bundy, from those who knew him, to those who chased him, and from those who mourned his many victims. The Trail of Ted Bundy: Digging Up the Untold Stories, is a journey back in time, to a world when Ted Bundy was killing young women and girls in the Pacific Northwest and beyond. You'll hear all the revealing stories; many of them coming to light for the first time. *wbp.bz/trailbundya*

Author of **THE TRAIL OF TED BUNDY**
and **THE BUNDY MURDERS**

KEVIN SULLIVAN

THE BUNDY
SECRETS
Hidden Files on America's
Worst Serial Killer

The Bundy Secrets: The hidden files of the manhunt to find and stop Ted Bundy, as well as the investigations into his depredations, gathered from official and unofficial sources from Washington to Florida, as well as contemporary interviews and author commentary to flesh out the details. A must-read for true crime students of Ted Bundy. *wbp.bz/ bundysecetsa*

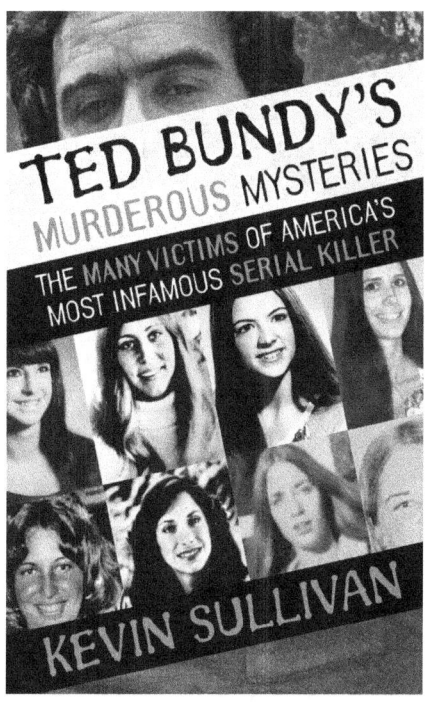

Ted Bundy's Murderous Mysteries: Written by the foremost authority on Ted Bundy, this latest examination of this brutal serial killer contains new, revealing, and never-before published interviews with those close to Bundy, close to his victims, and a potential victim who barely escaped his clutches. *wbp.bz/tbmma*

www.ingramcontent.com/pod-product-compliance
Lightning Source LLC
Chambersburg PA
CBHW071154120626
46546CB00006B/2266